For as he thinketh in his heart, so is he...
Proverbs 23:7

Written by
Karen Porter and Dr. Martha Joseph Watts

Illustrated by
Karen Porter

Emotion Mandalas

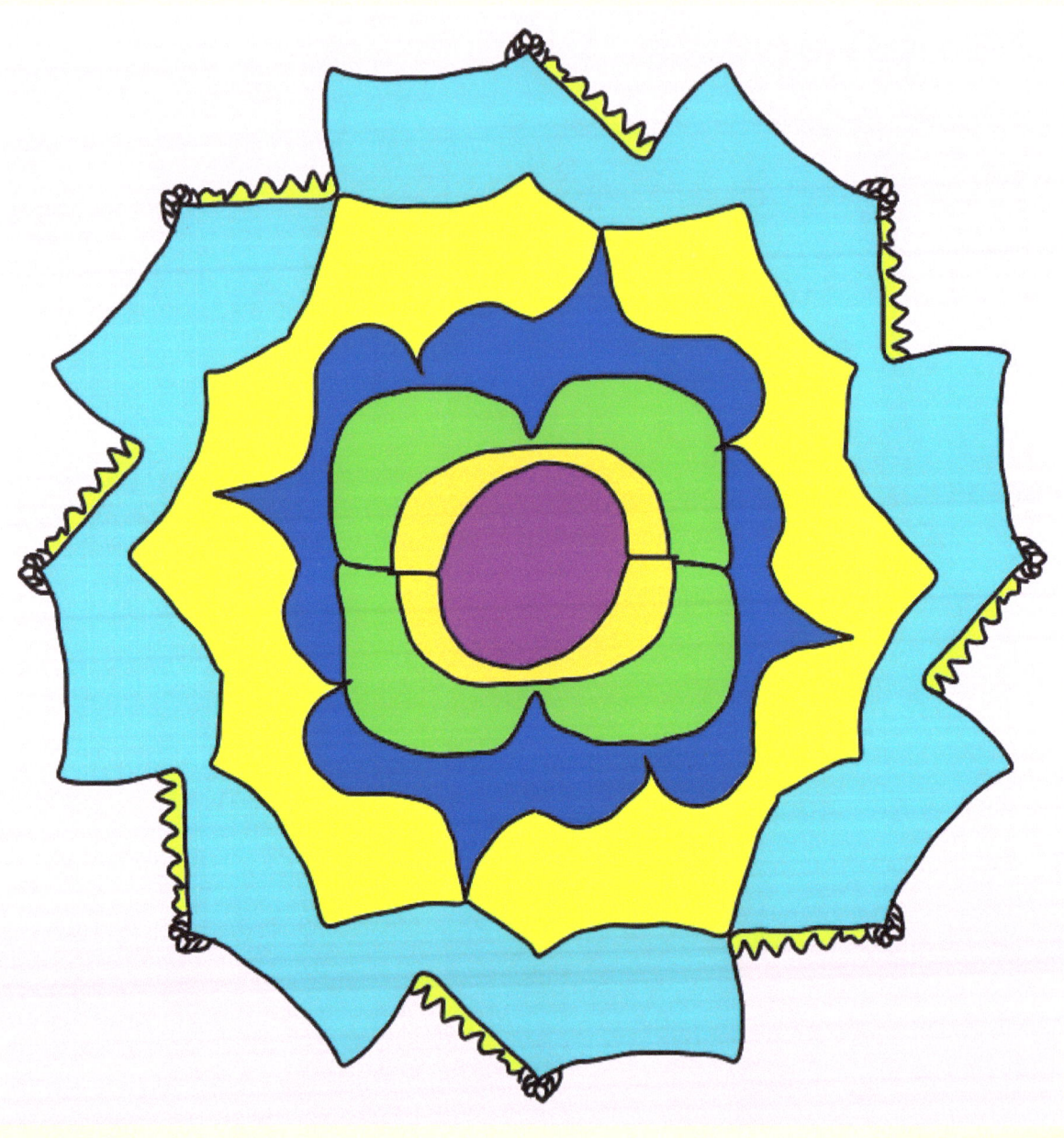

Copyright 2020 by Everfield Press
ISBN: 978-1-946785-23-7

This Book is Dedicated

To

Your Inner Voice

This nonfiction book contains illustrations and definitions of 25 emotions that will help express feelings.
KAREN PORTER
Copyright © 2020 Karen Porter., Everfield Press, Florida. All rights reserved. No part of this book shall be reproduced or transmitted in any form or means, electronic, mechanical, magnetic, photographic including photocopying, recording or by any information storage and retrieval system, without prior written permission of the author.
All rights reserved.
ISBN: 978-1-946785-23-7

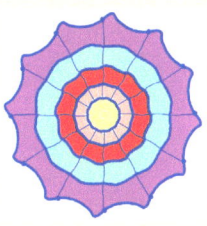

Foreword and Note to Users

The definition of mandalas may vary, but there are a few things about them that are constant-- circular, symbolic, spiritual, and focuses on self- unity. Although, the mandala may be viewed as a religious symbol, it may be used for a variety of significant purposes, one of which is as a tool to encourage social emotional awareness.
As time elapses and the world becomes more tech-focused, we notice that children, students and even adults find it difficult to "feel what they are feeling" in simple terms they are not able to pause long enough to feel, acknowledge and express what they feel.

Experts in the field of social emotional learning warn that we need to maintain good mental health among students. Educators must be prepared to teach children how to cope with feelings brought on by the pandemic in the same way we do for natural disasters and school unrest.

Hence the purpose of this book is to provide vocabulary to encourage individuals big or small to pause, connect with their feelings, acknowledge them, feel free to express them, and make decisions about managing or regulating those feelings in ways that encourage self-wellness and mindfulness.

More recently, our schools and places of worship have become places of violent attacks and levels of anxiety in classrooms have risen and instructors are at most times helpless, particularly, in settings where the number of students requiring emotional support out-weigh the number of professional support available.

Therefore, it is our hope that educators at home, in schools, and in communities can utilize this Mandala book as a safe place to encourage students to explore their feelings and develop the courage to express them with art.

Take a pause, replicate the last page of this book, or get the coloring book version and add shapes, lines, and colors to express how you feel.

You may then use your work to create poetry, stories, or art. See an example on page 27.

Feeling
To have an emotional state or reaction.

Everyone has feelings.

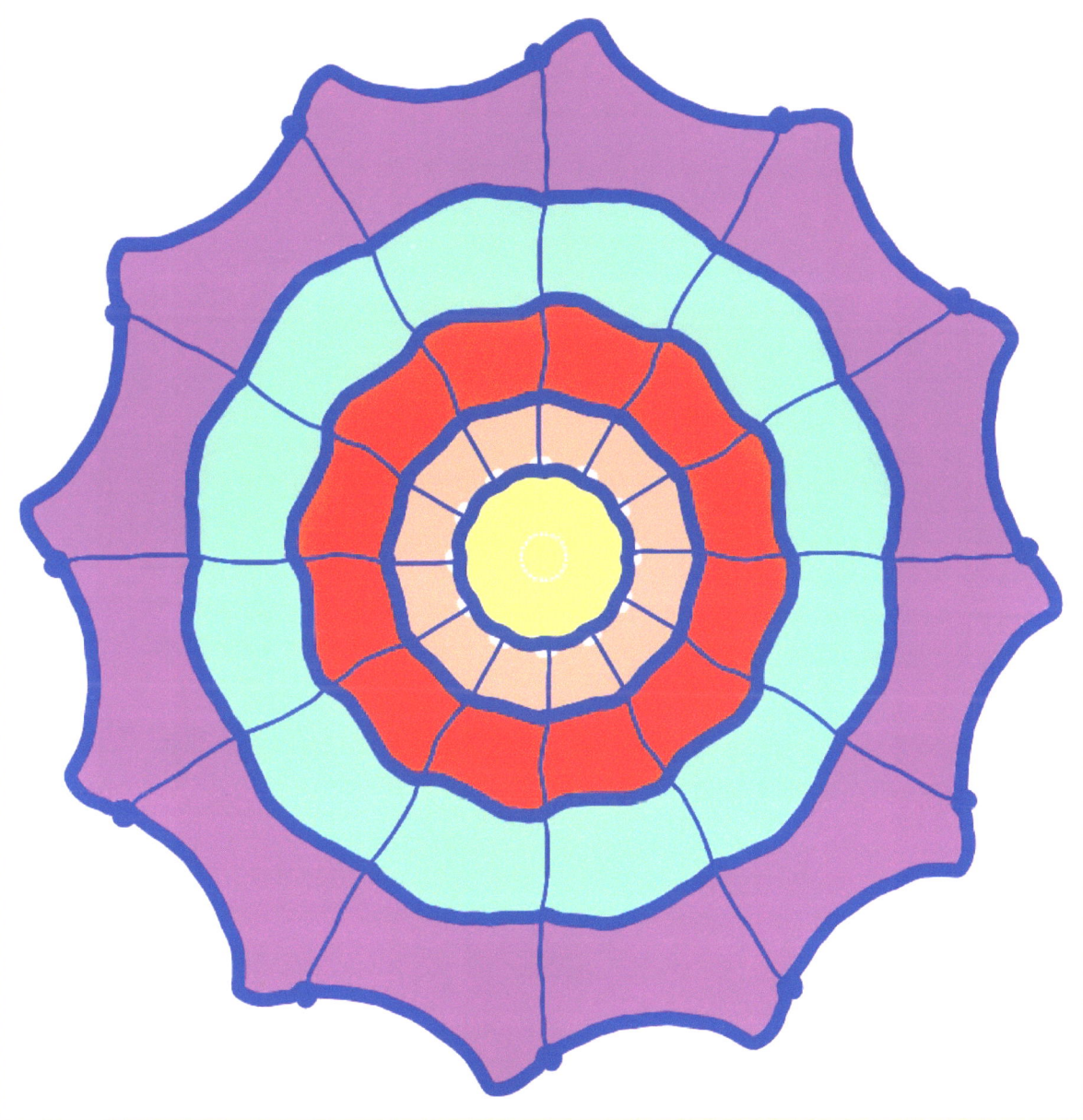

What happens inside to make us feel?

Confident

To feel like you can do anything well.

Sometimes you look confident.

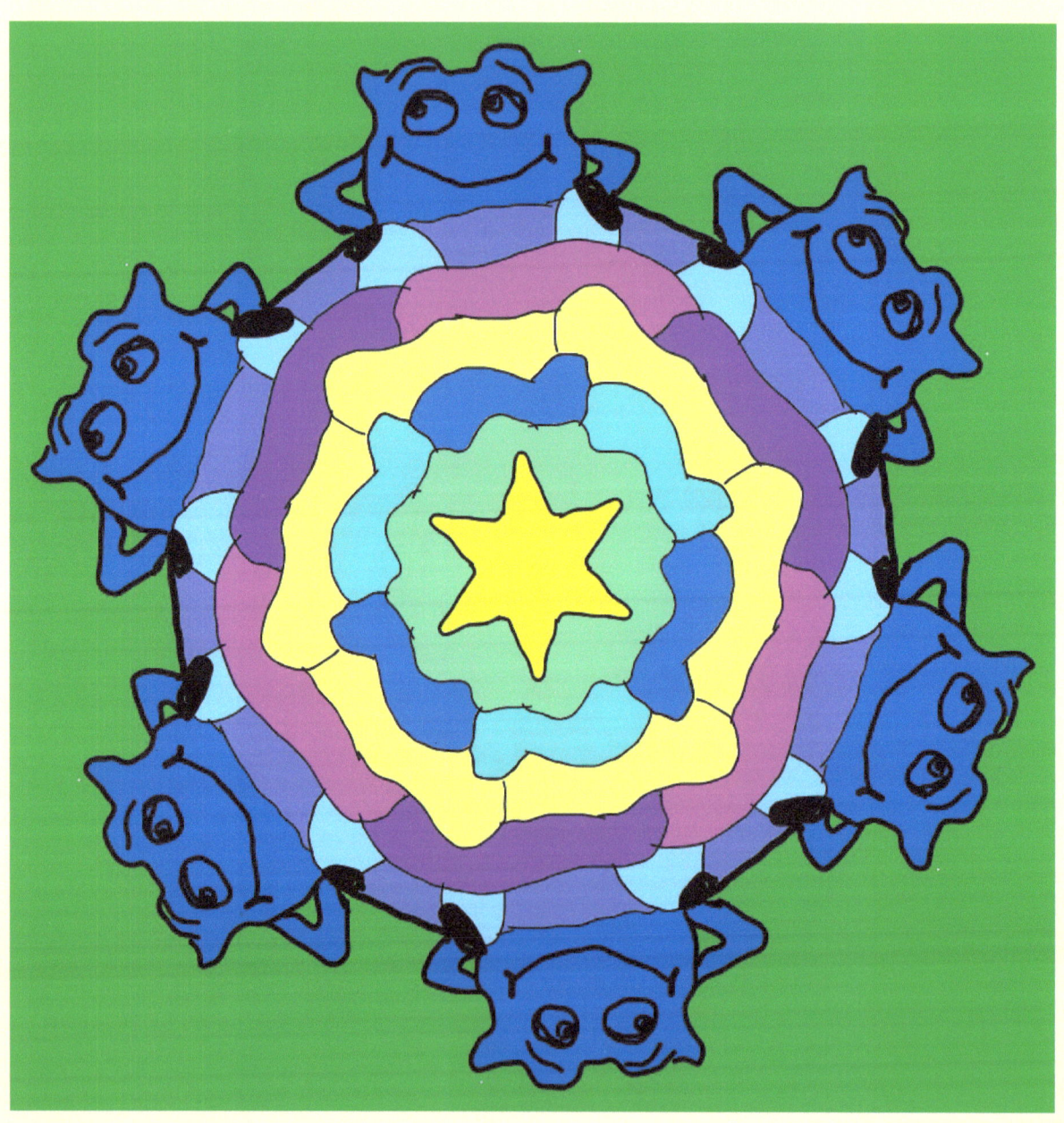

What happens inside to make you look confident?

Afraid

To feel like something can hurt you.

Sometimes you look afraid.

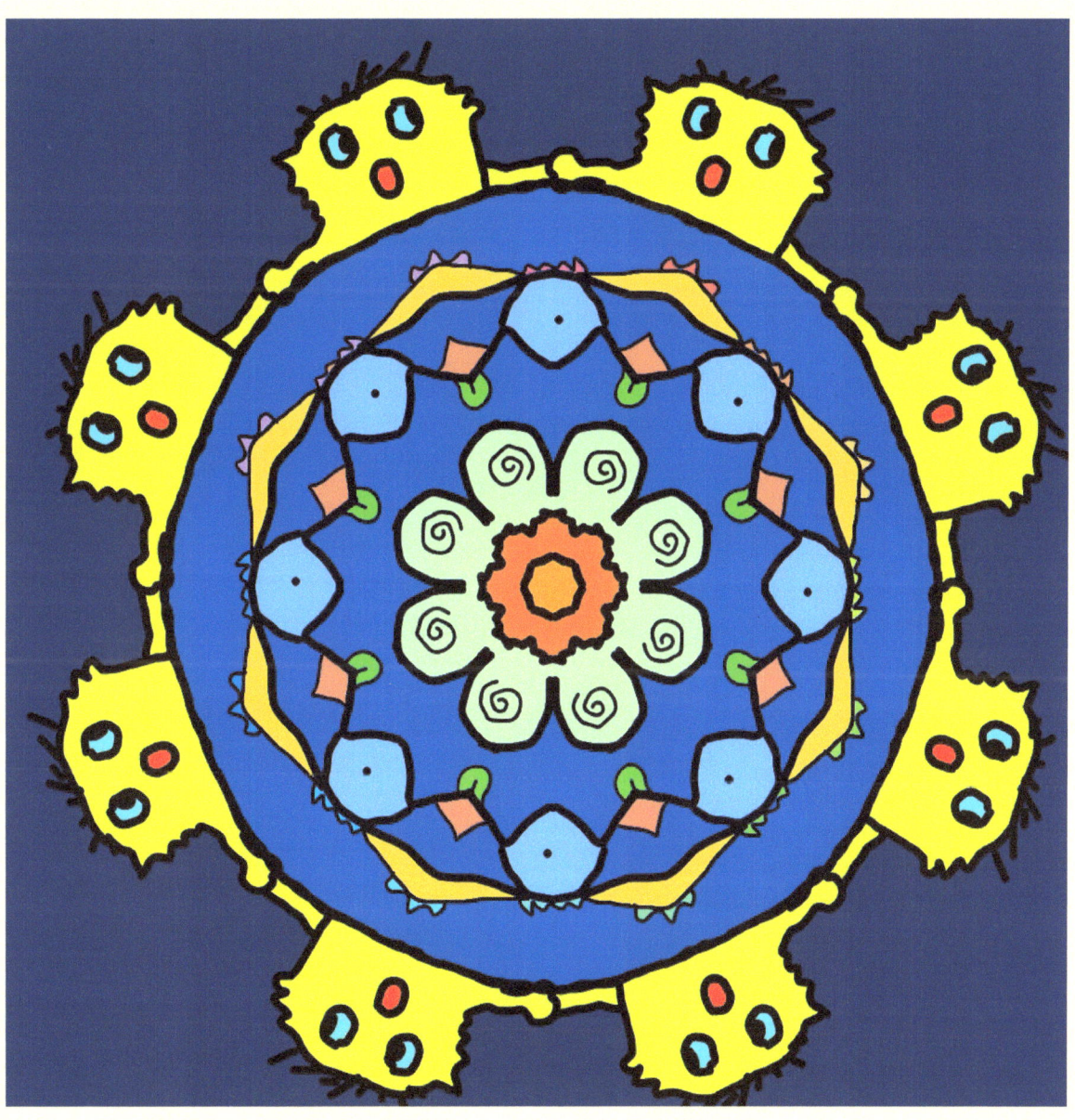

What happens inside to make you look afraid?

Excited

To feel everything is awesome.

Sometimes you look excited on the outside!

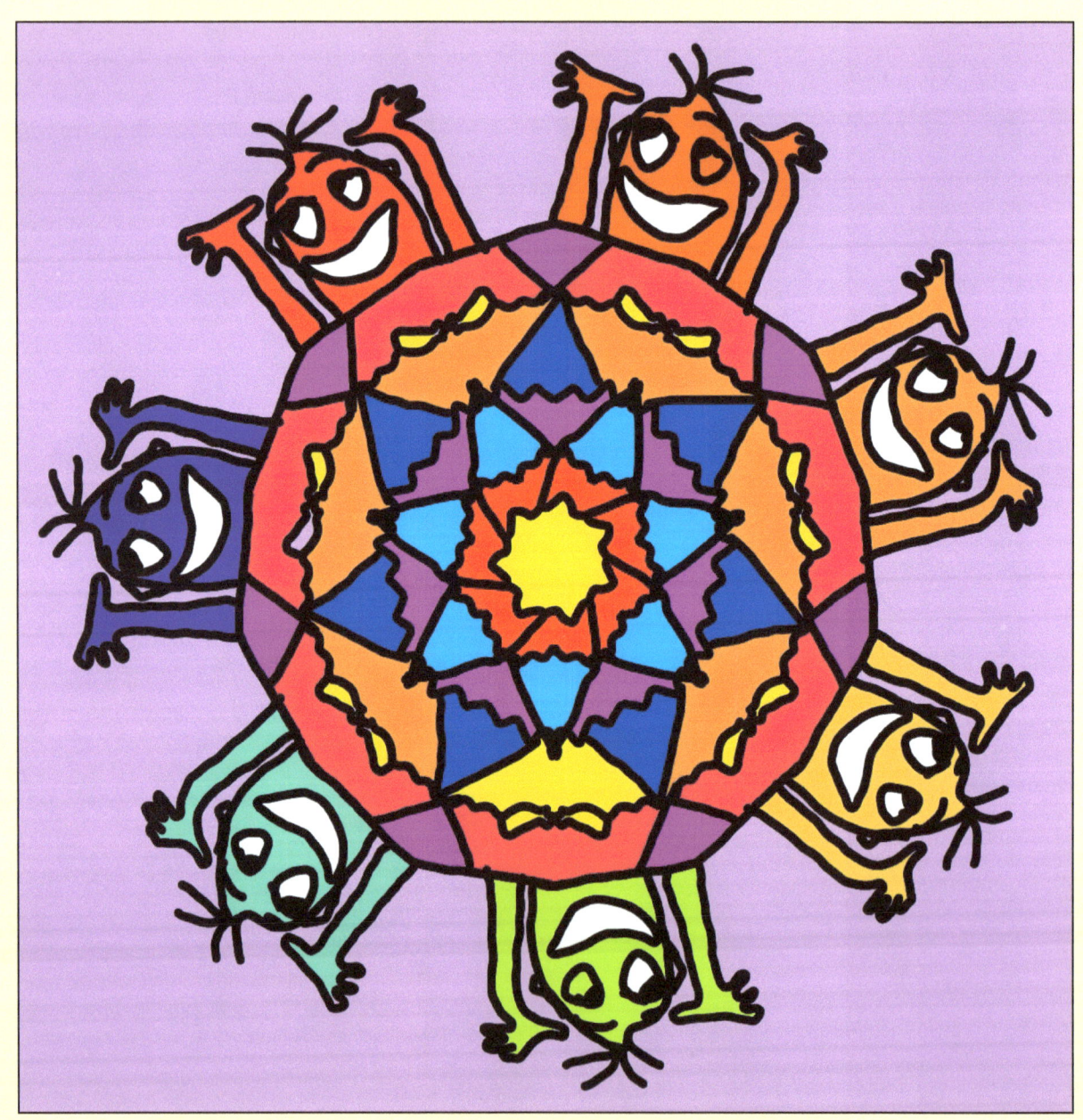

What happens inside to make you look excited?

Angry

To feel like somebody did something wrong to you.

Sometimes you look angry on the outside.

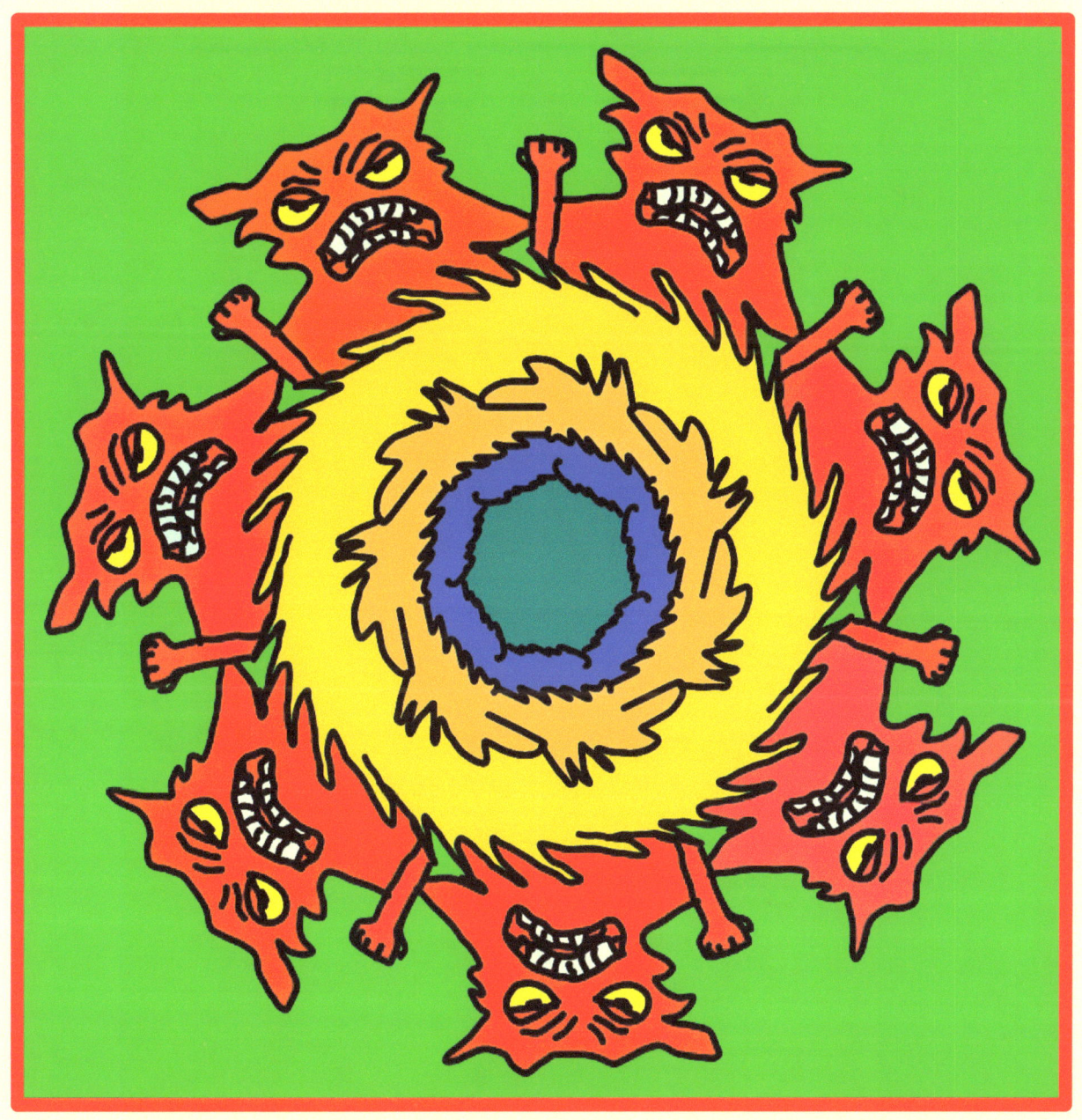

What happens inside to make you look angry?

Happy
To feel glad like you want to smile.

Sometimes you look happy on the outside.

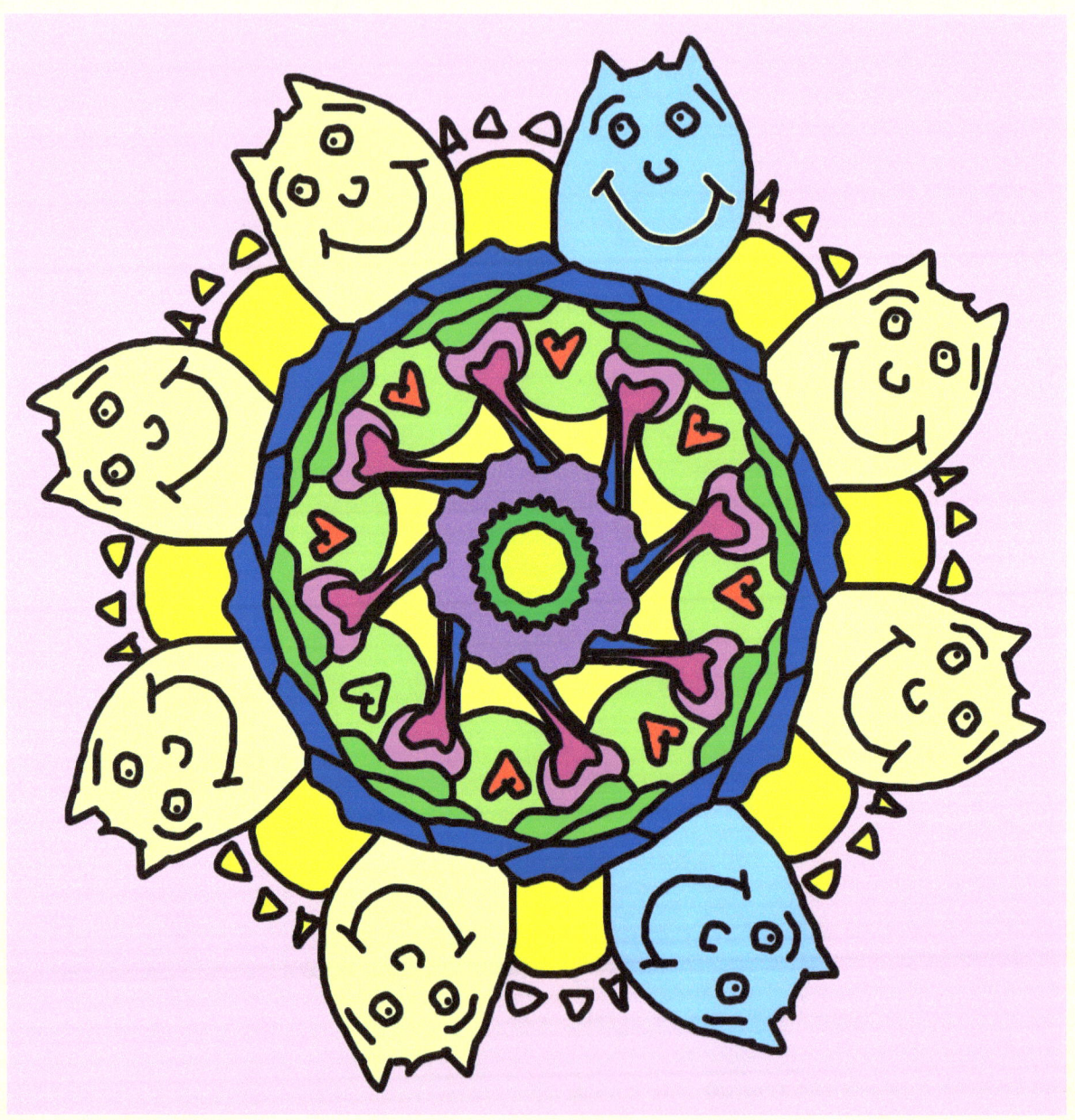

What happens inside to make you look happy?

Bored

To feel like you don't care, or
don't want to do anything.
Sometimes you look bored on the outside.

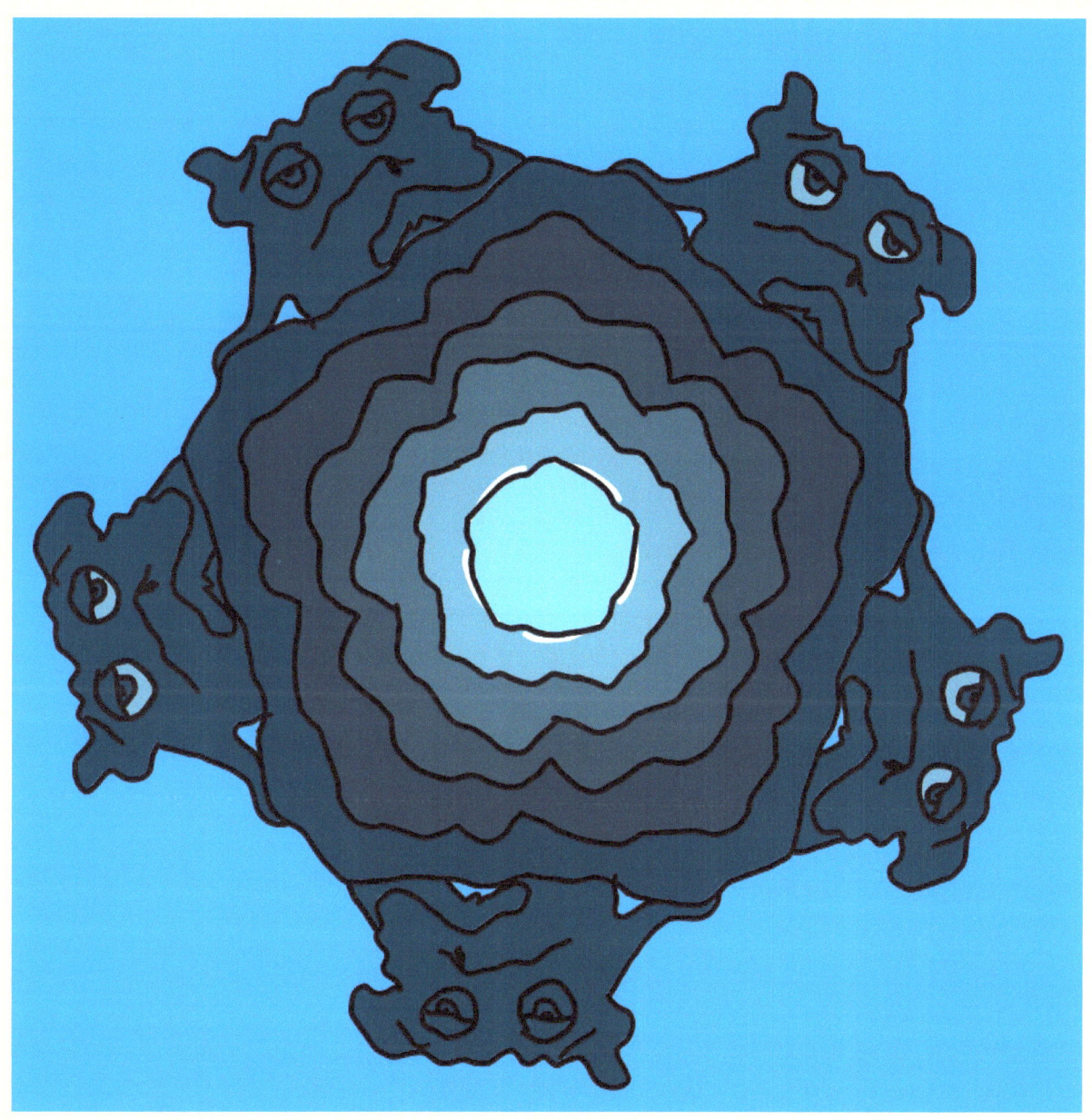

What happens inside to make you
look bored?

Hopeful

To feel like things are going to get better.

Sometimes you look hopeful on the outside!

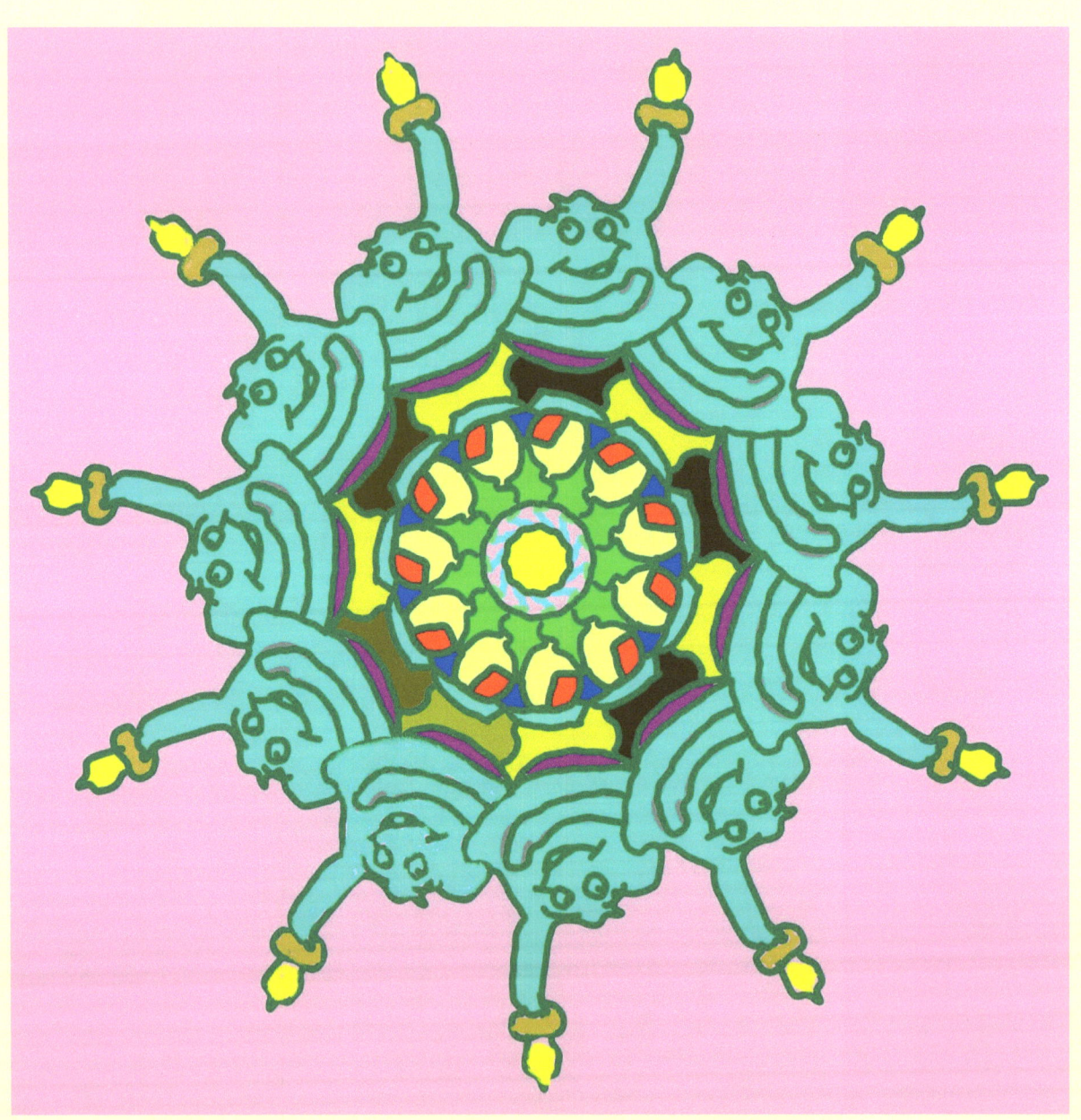

What happens inside to make you look hopeful?

Confused

To feel unsure about something

Sometimes you look confused.

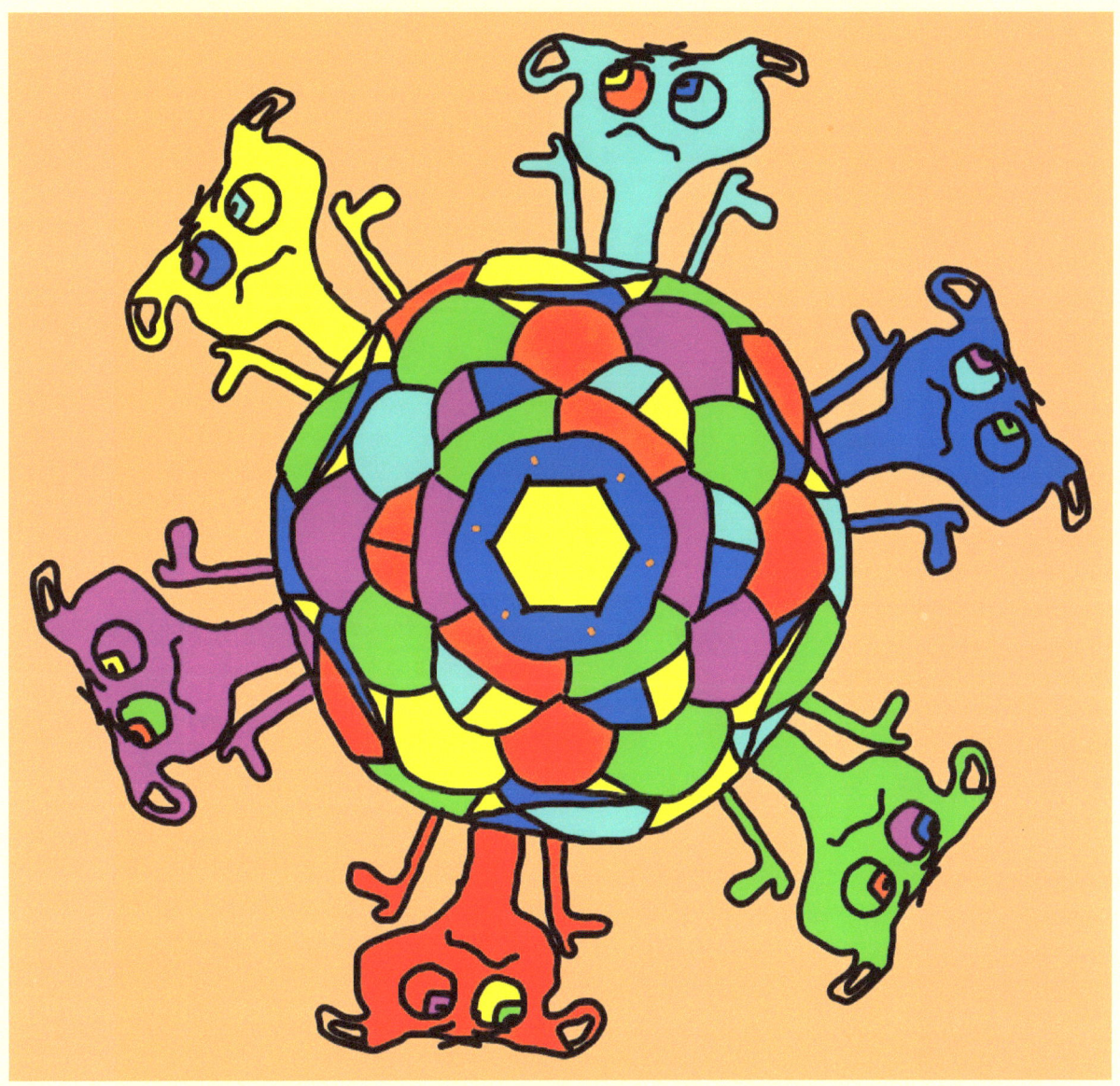

What happens inside to make you look confused?

Disappointed

To feel like you can not get what you want.

Sometimes you look disappointed.

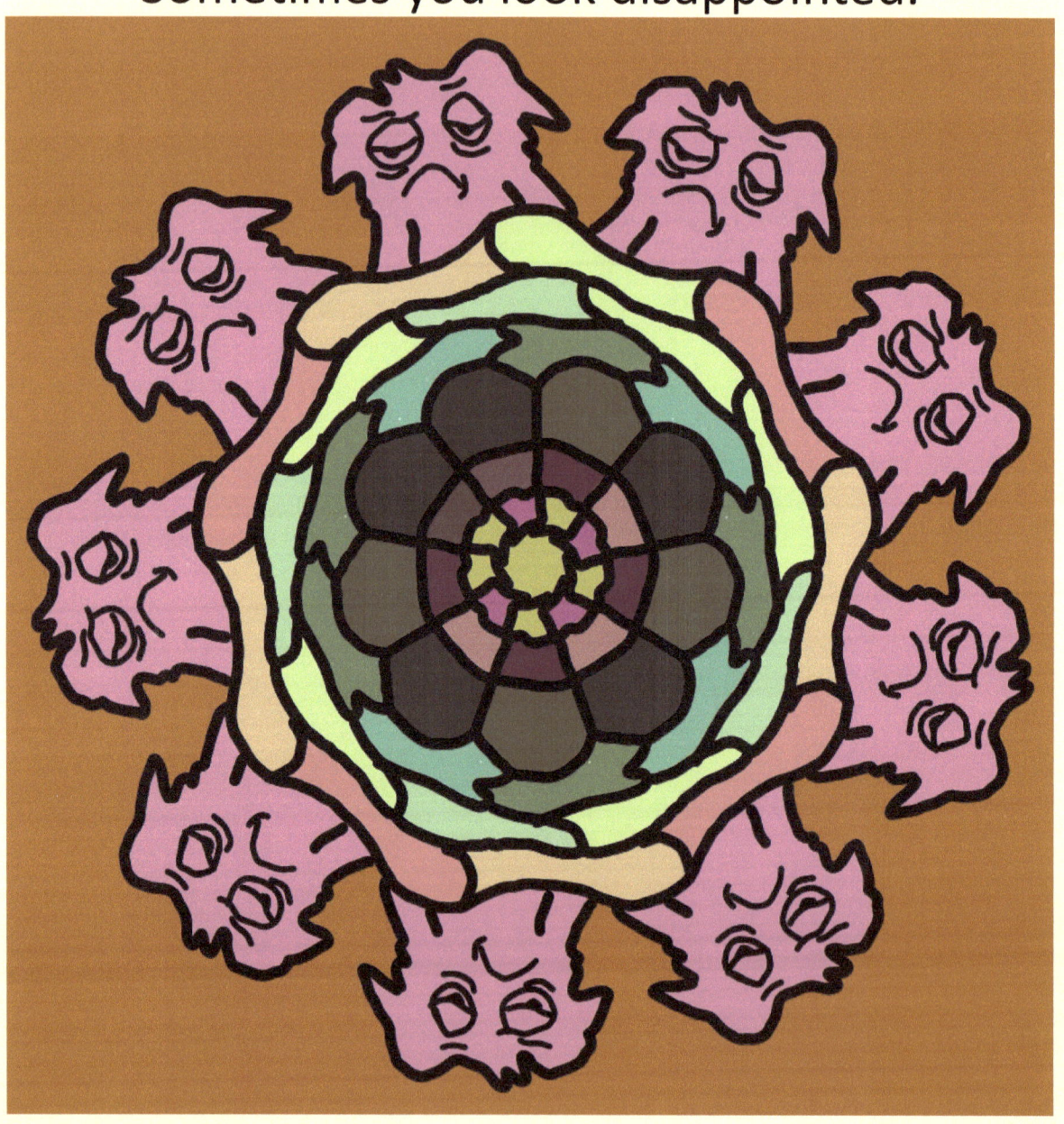

What happens inside to make you look disappointed?

10

Embarrassed
To feel ashamed.

Sometimes you look embarrassed.

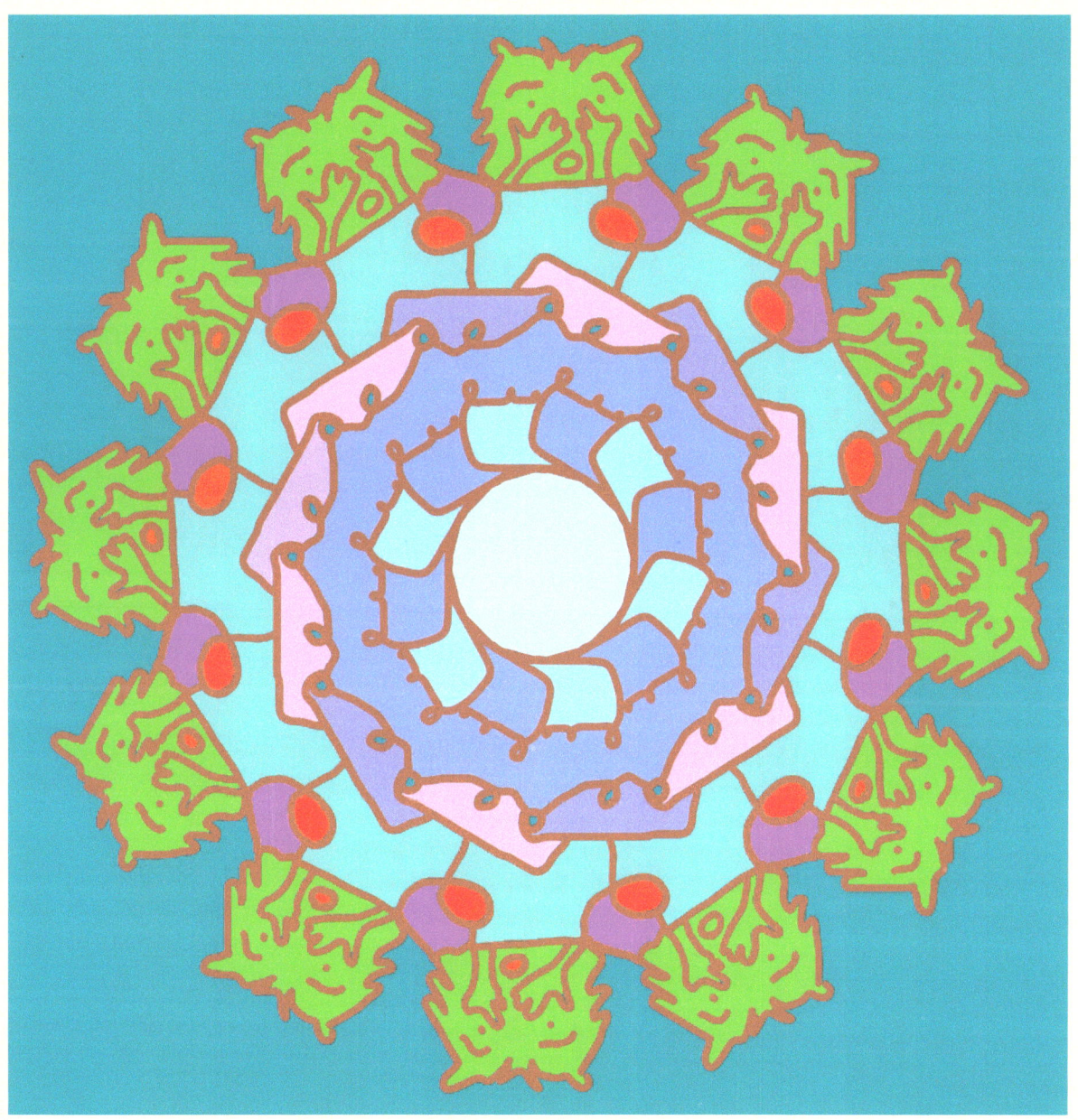

What happens inside to make you look embarrassed?

11

Shy

To feel like you do not want others to notice you

Sometimes you look shy on the outside.

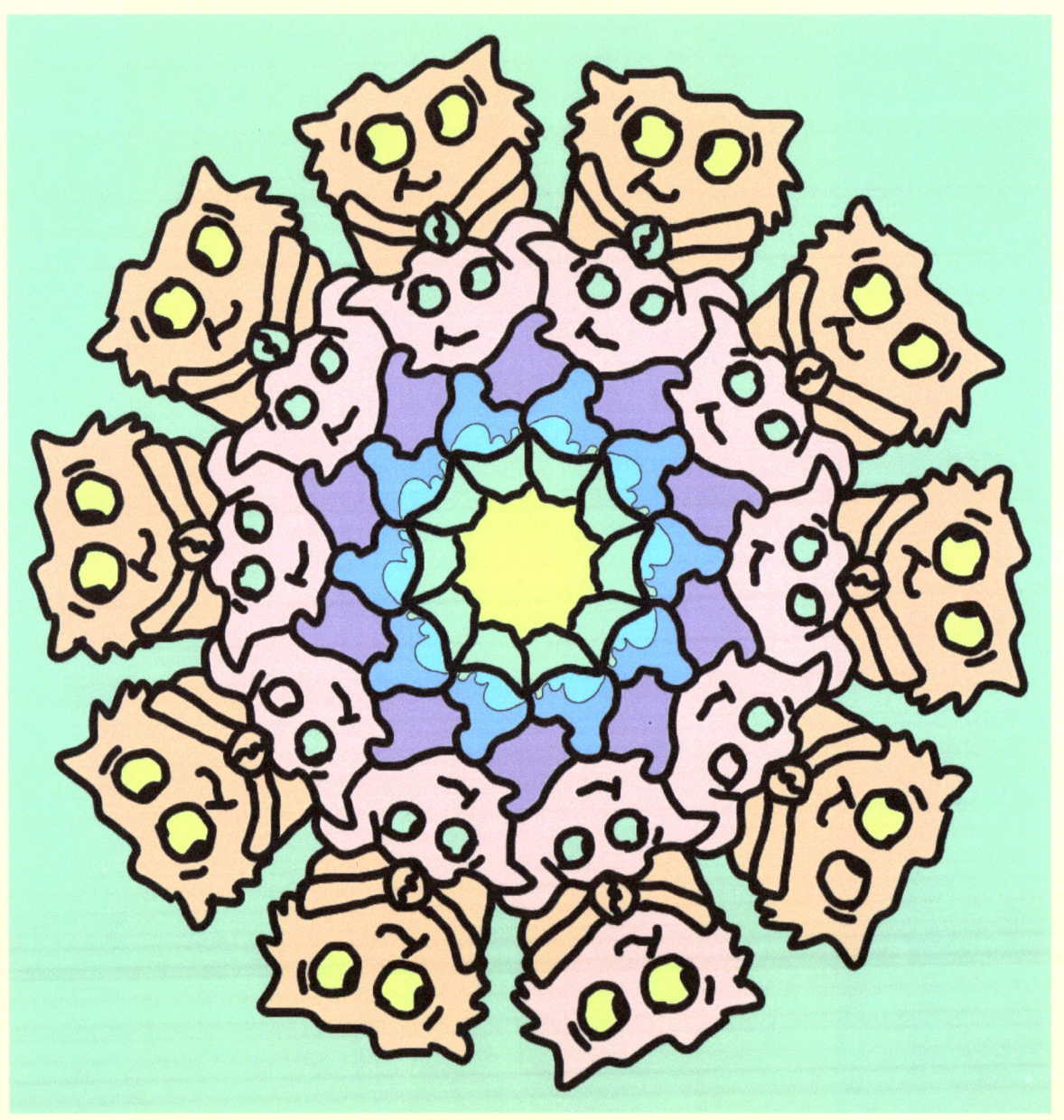

What happens inside to make you
look shy?

12

Frustrated

To feel stuck in a problem you can not fix.

Sometimes you look frustrated on the outside.

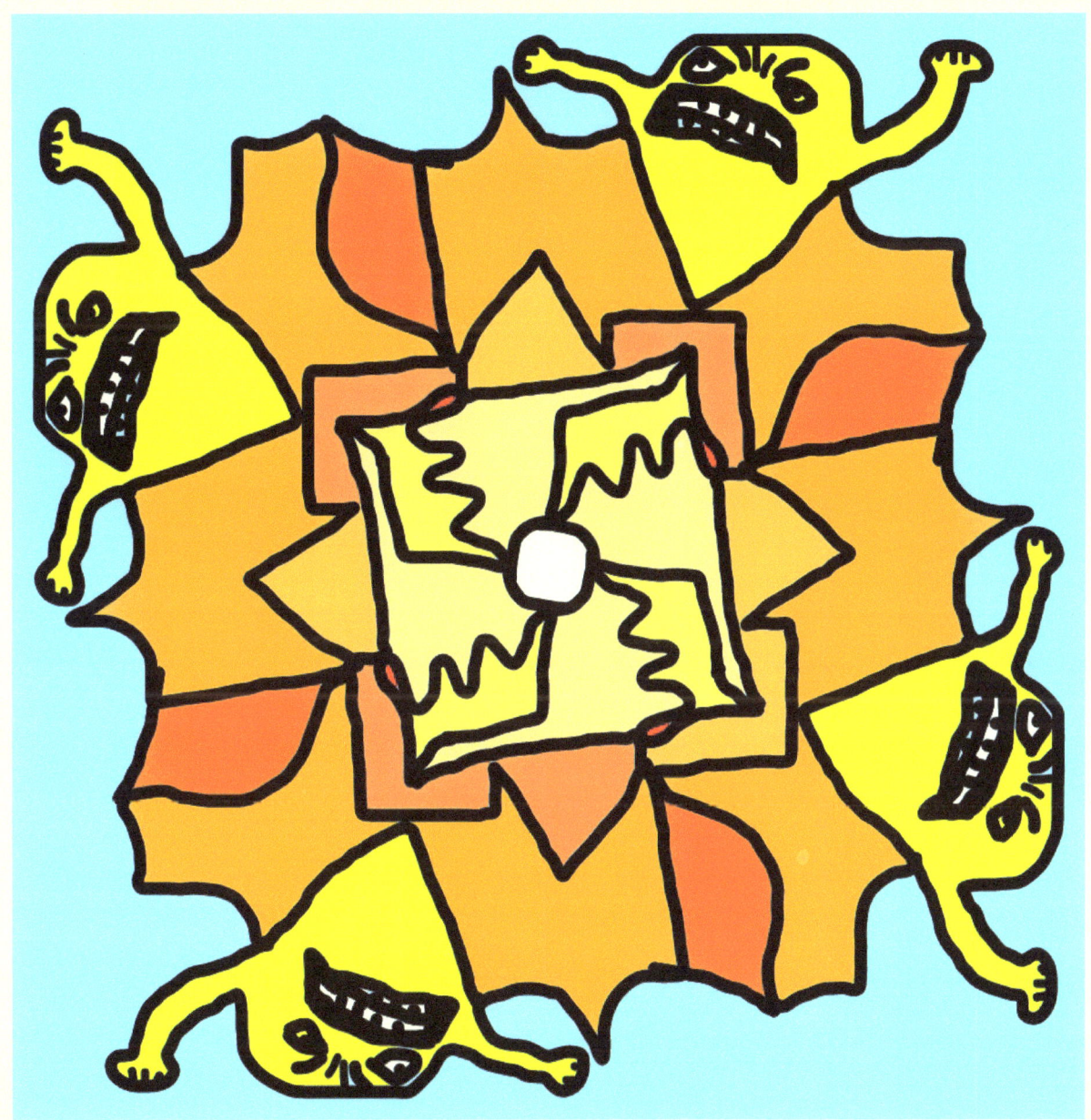

What happens inside to make you look frustrated?

Grumpy

To feel bothered by others.

Sometimes you look grumpy on the outside.

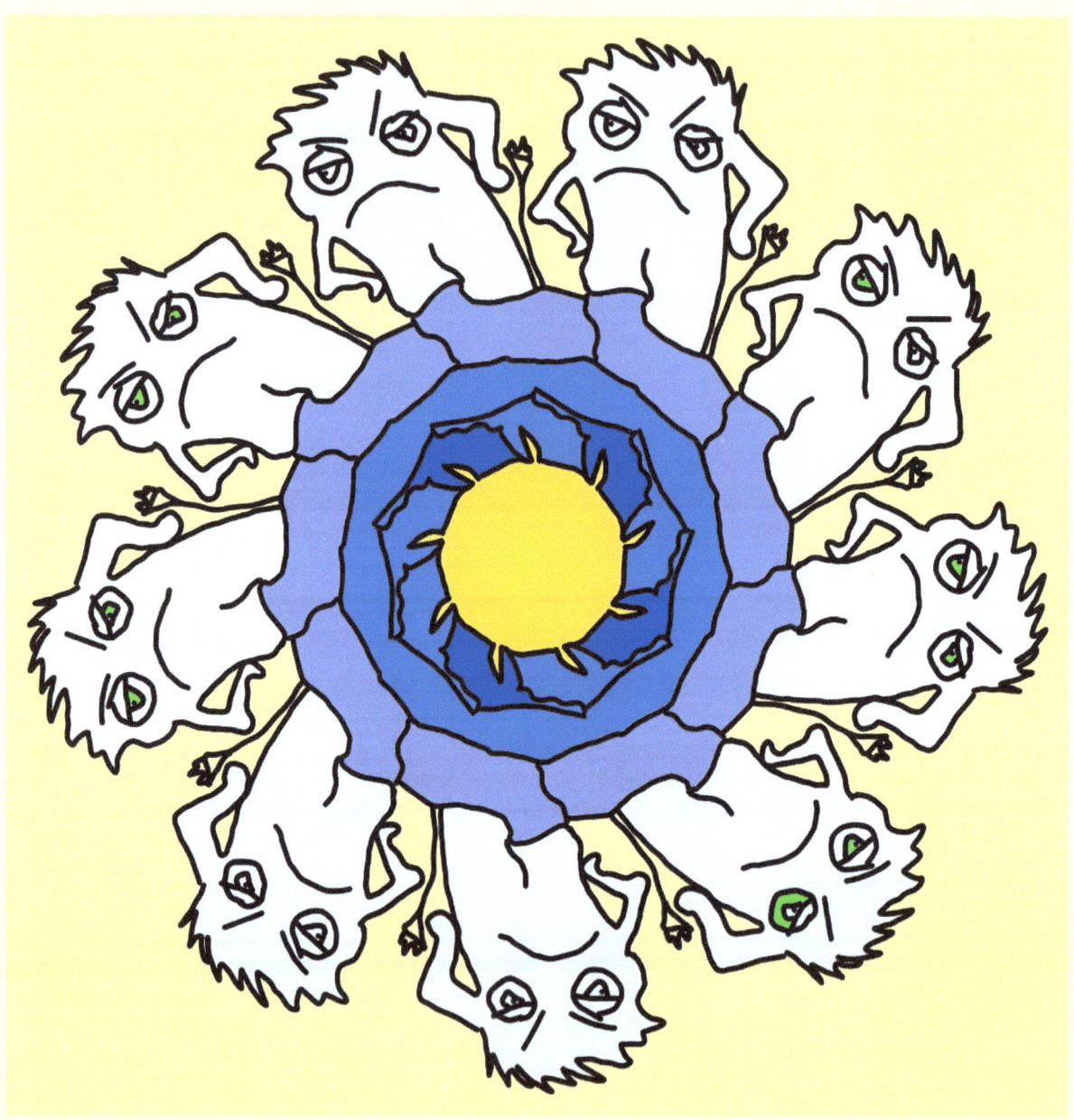

What happens inside to make you look grumpy?

Guilty

To feel as if it is our fault.

Sometimes you look guilty on the outside.

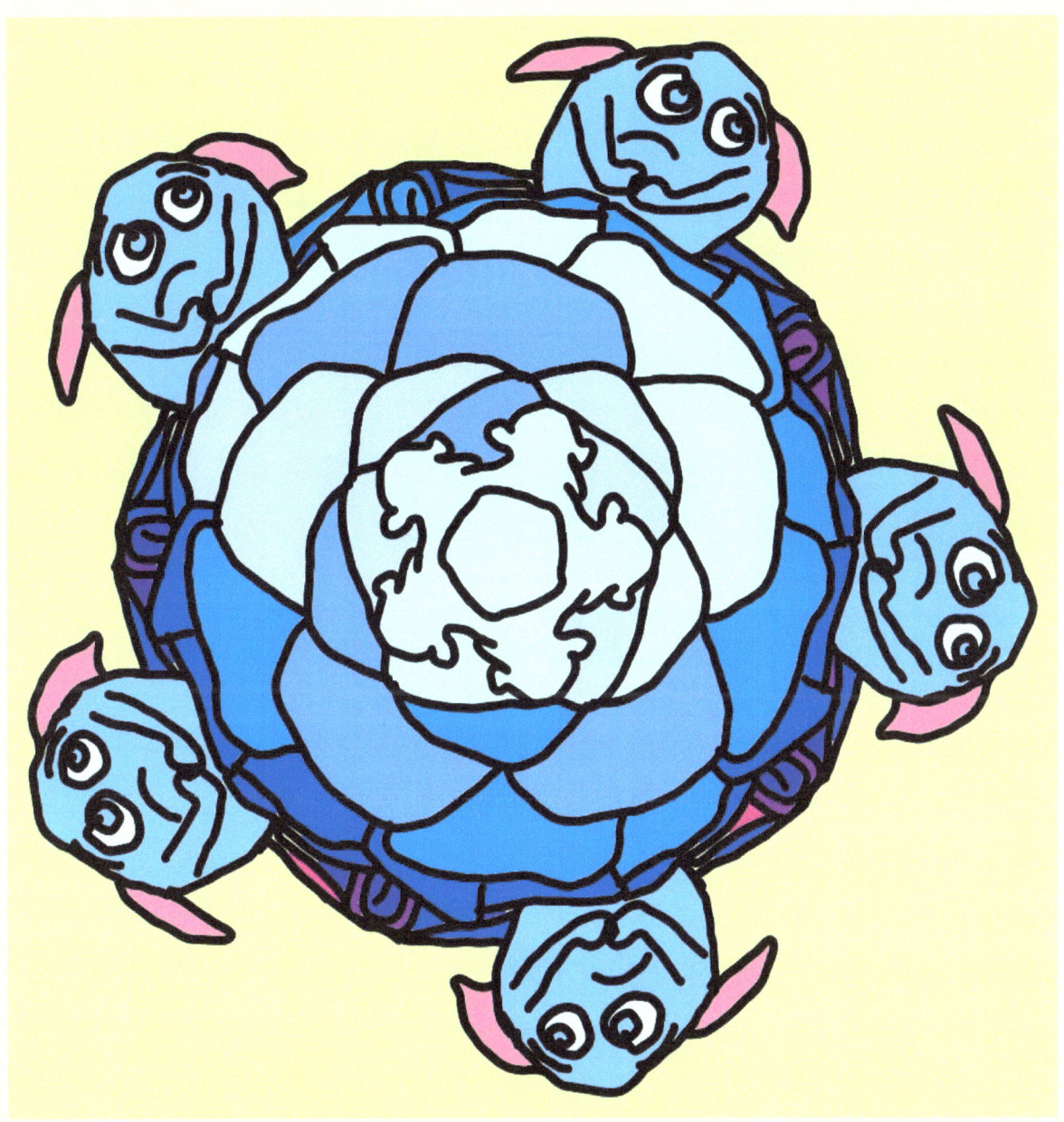

What happens inside to make you look guilty?

Sad

To feel loss, pain, and unhappiness.

Sometimes you look sad on the outside.

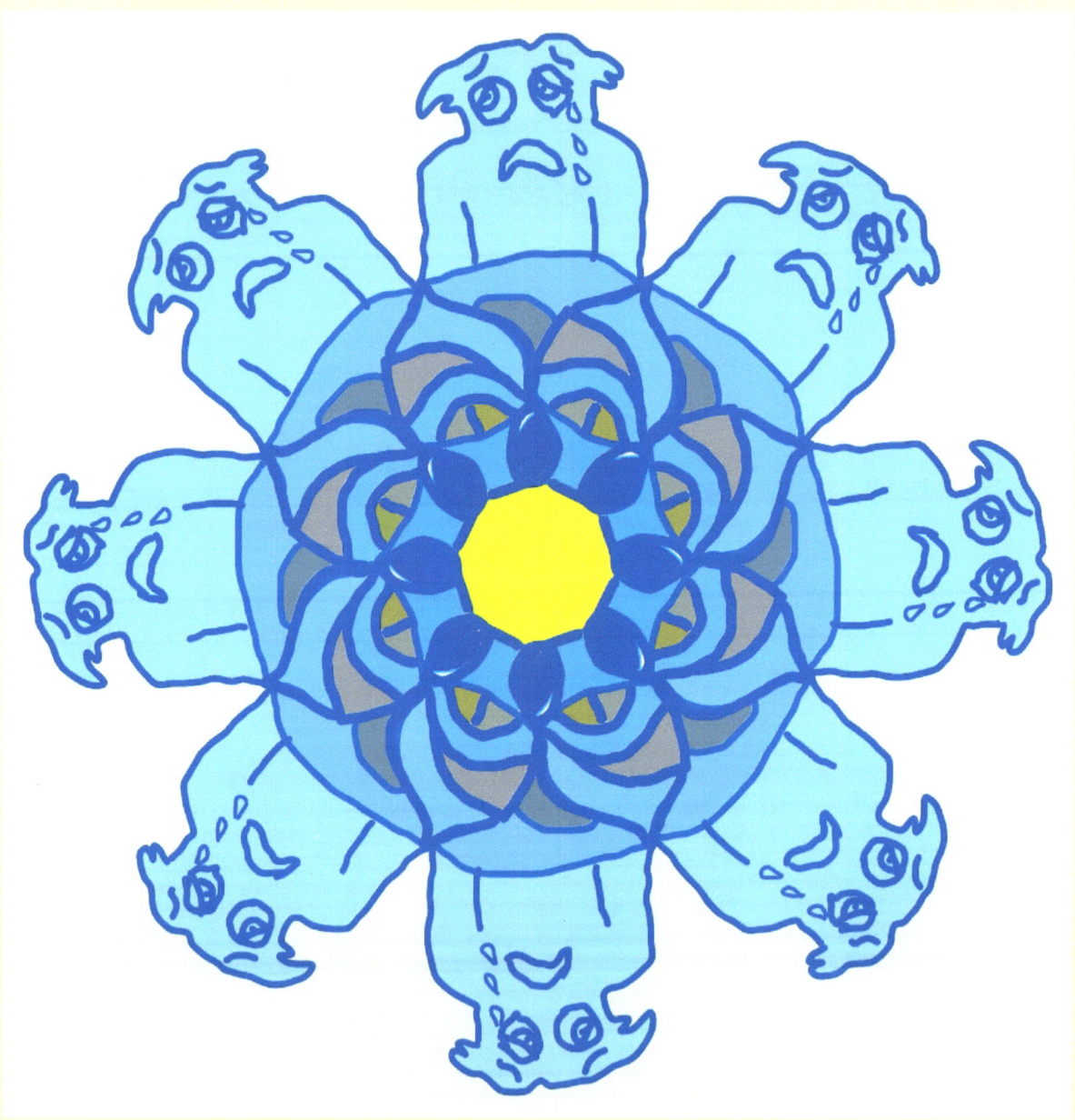

What happens inside to make you look sad?

16

Hungry

To feel a need for food.

Sometimes you look hungry on the outside.

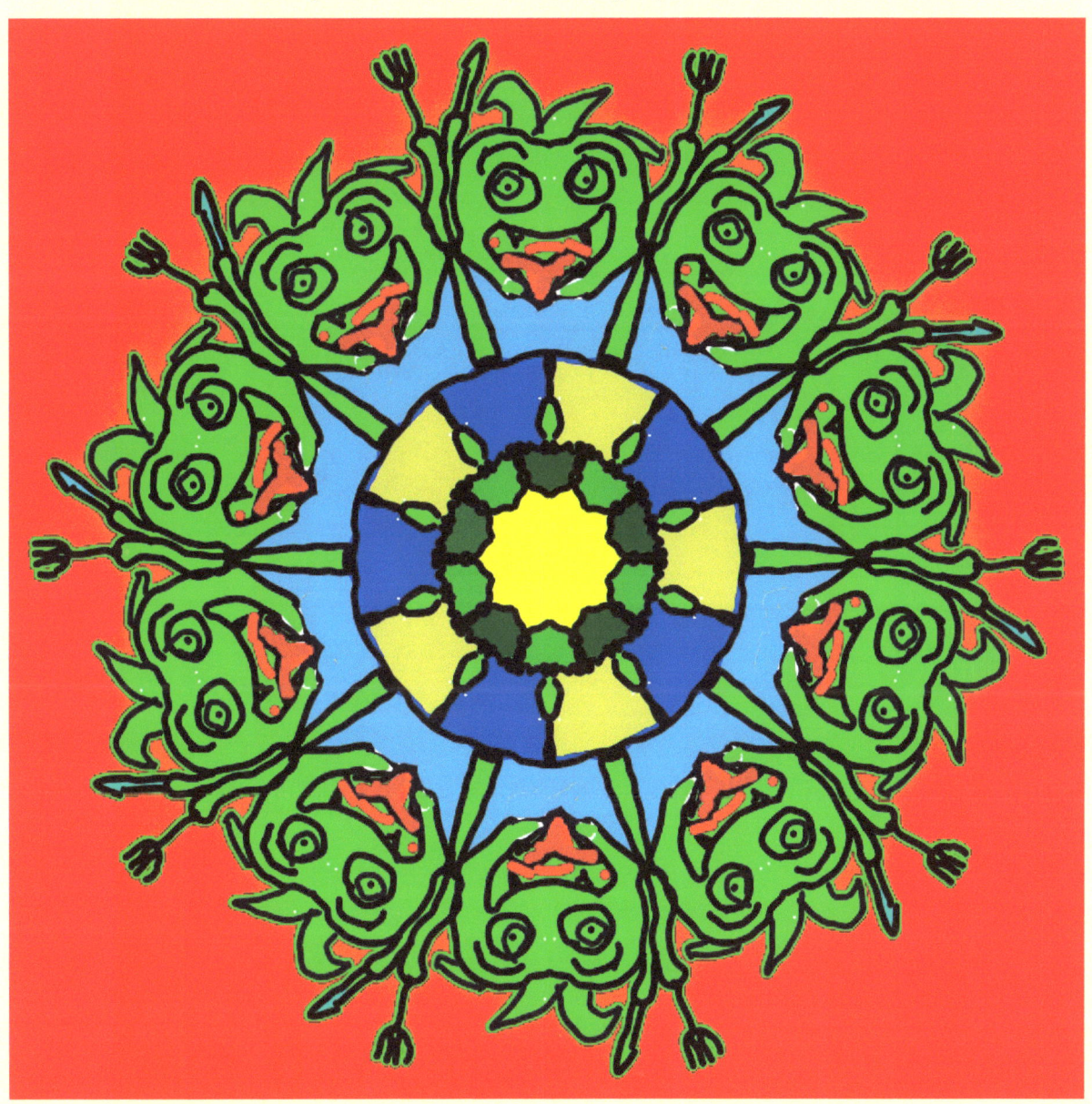

What happens inside to make you look hungry?

Sick

To feel ill like when our body hurts.

Sometimes you look sick on the outside.

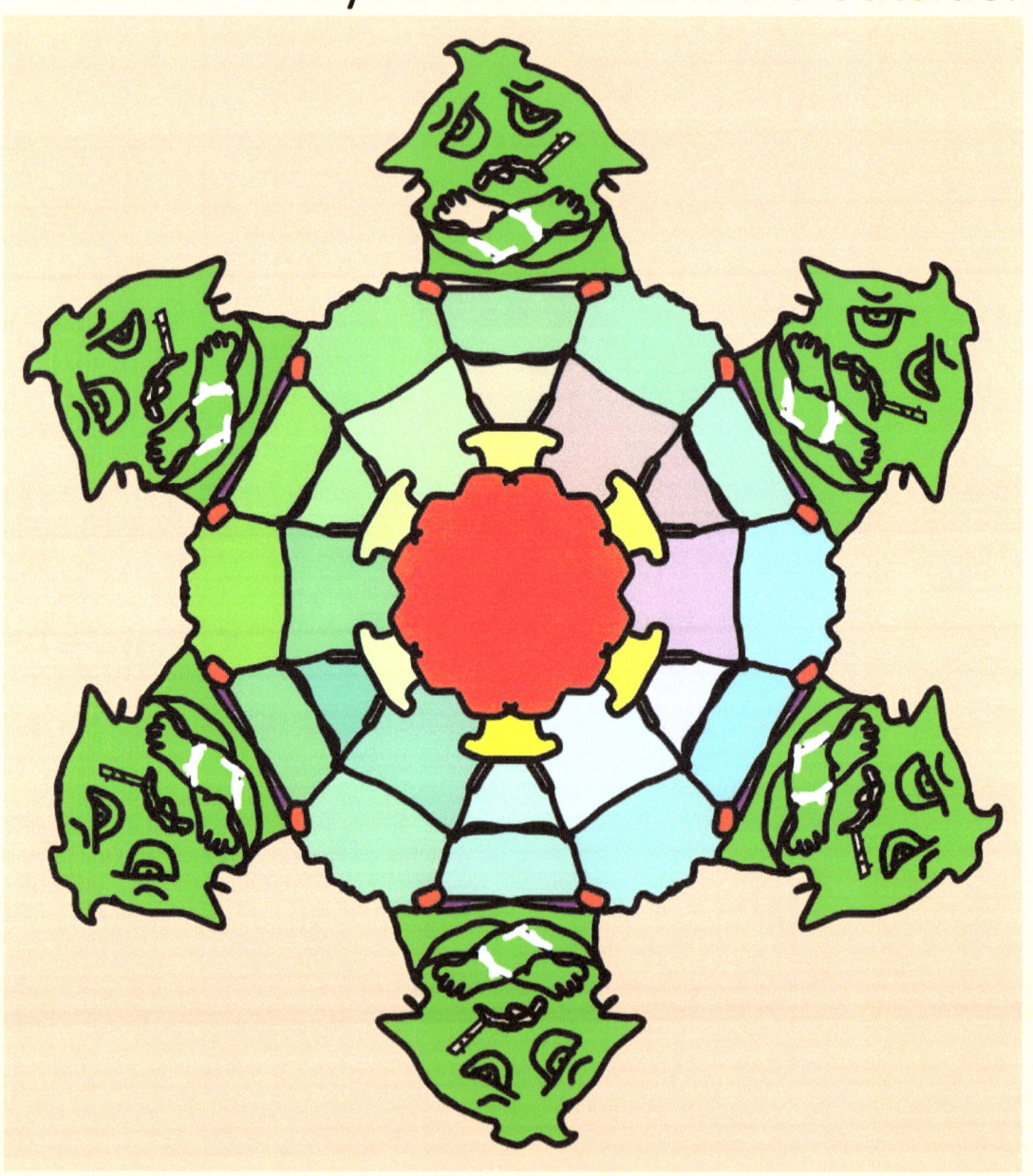

What happens inside to make you look sick?

Worried

To feel afraid about what could go wrong.

Sometimes you look worried on the outside.

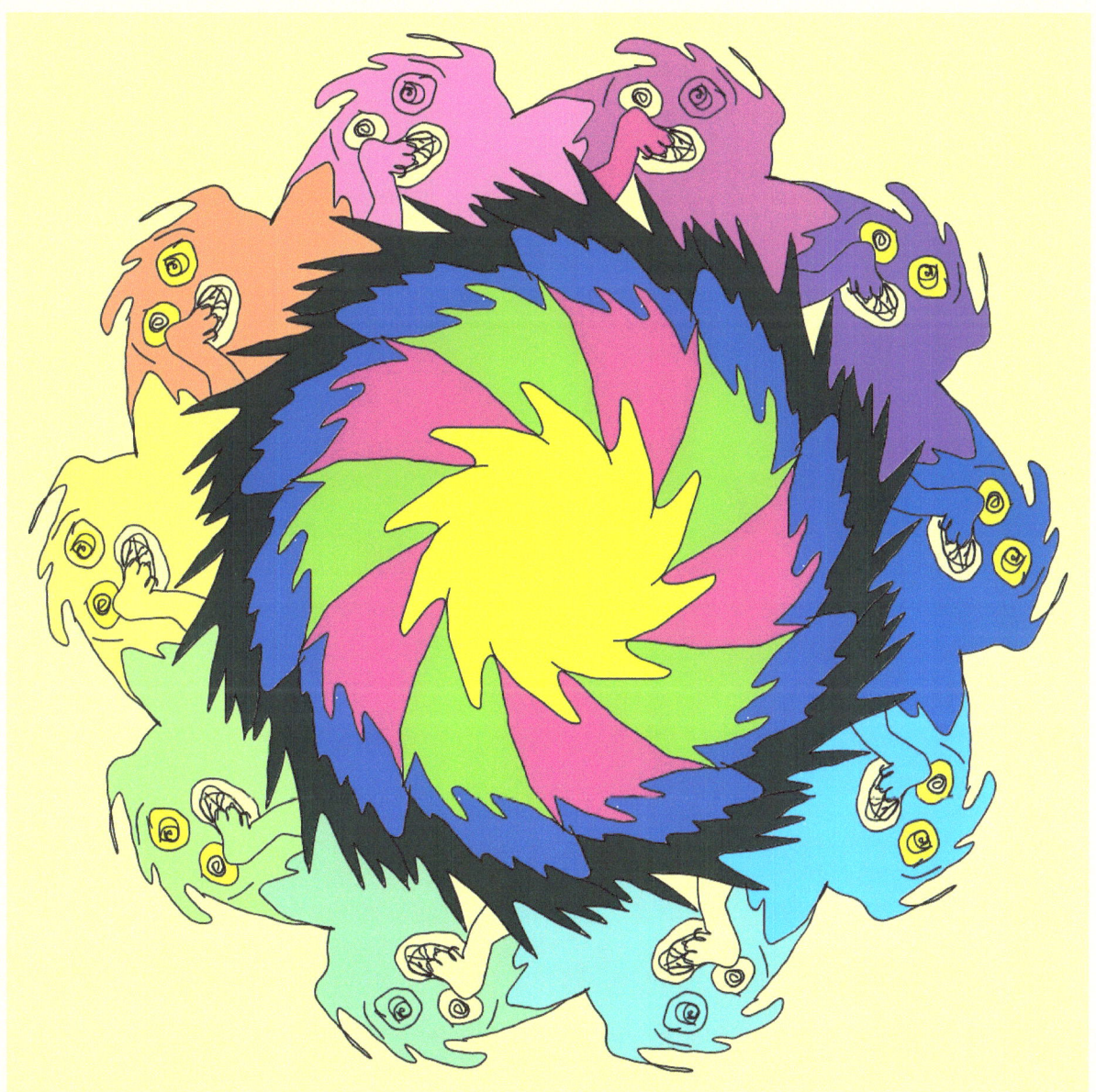

What happens inside to make you look worried?

19

Stressed
To feel bothered all the time.

Sometimes you look stressed on the outside.

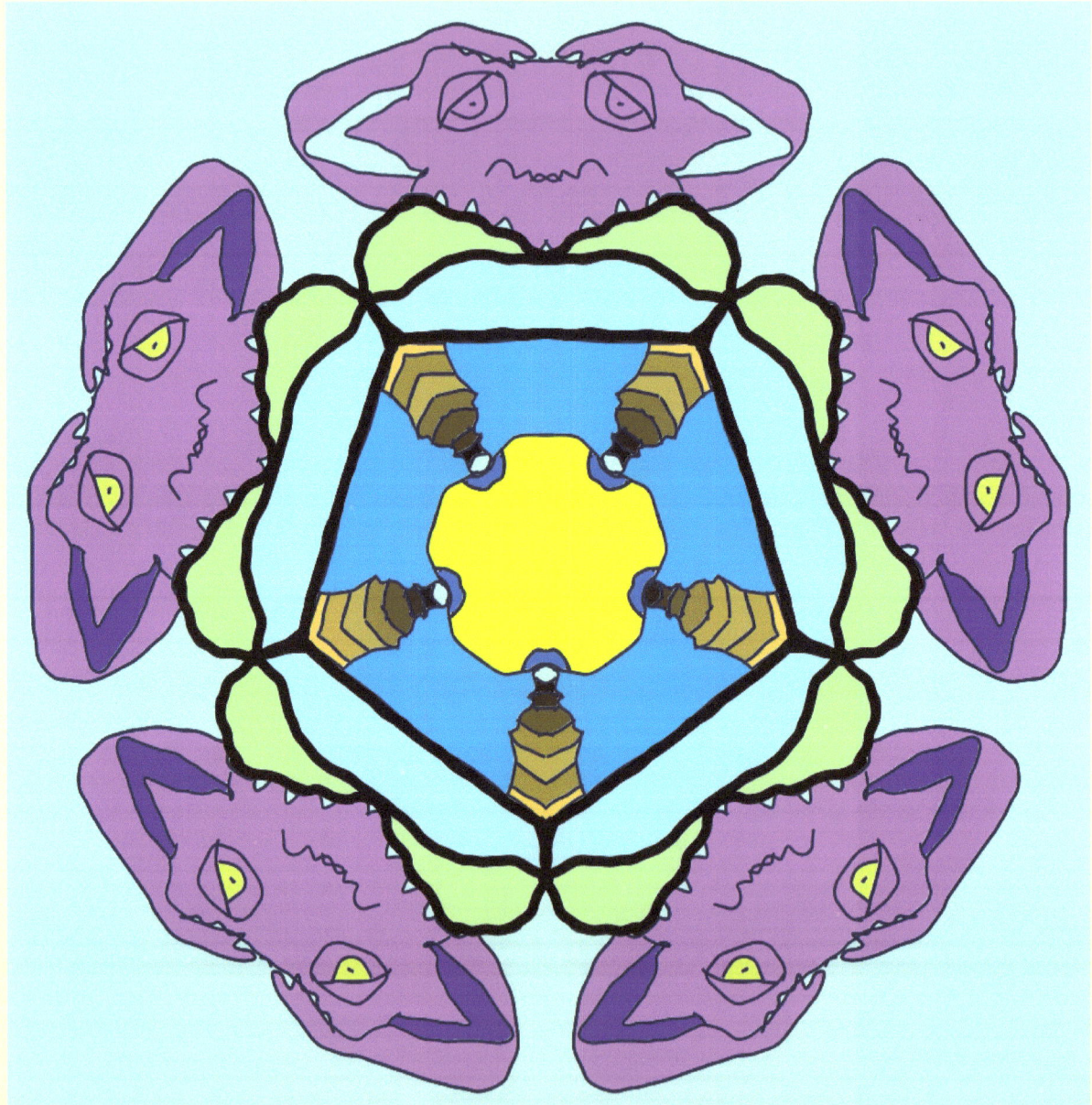

What happens inside to make you look stressed?

Sleepy

To feel tired like you want to lay down.

Sometimes you look sleepy on the outside.

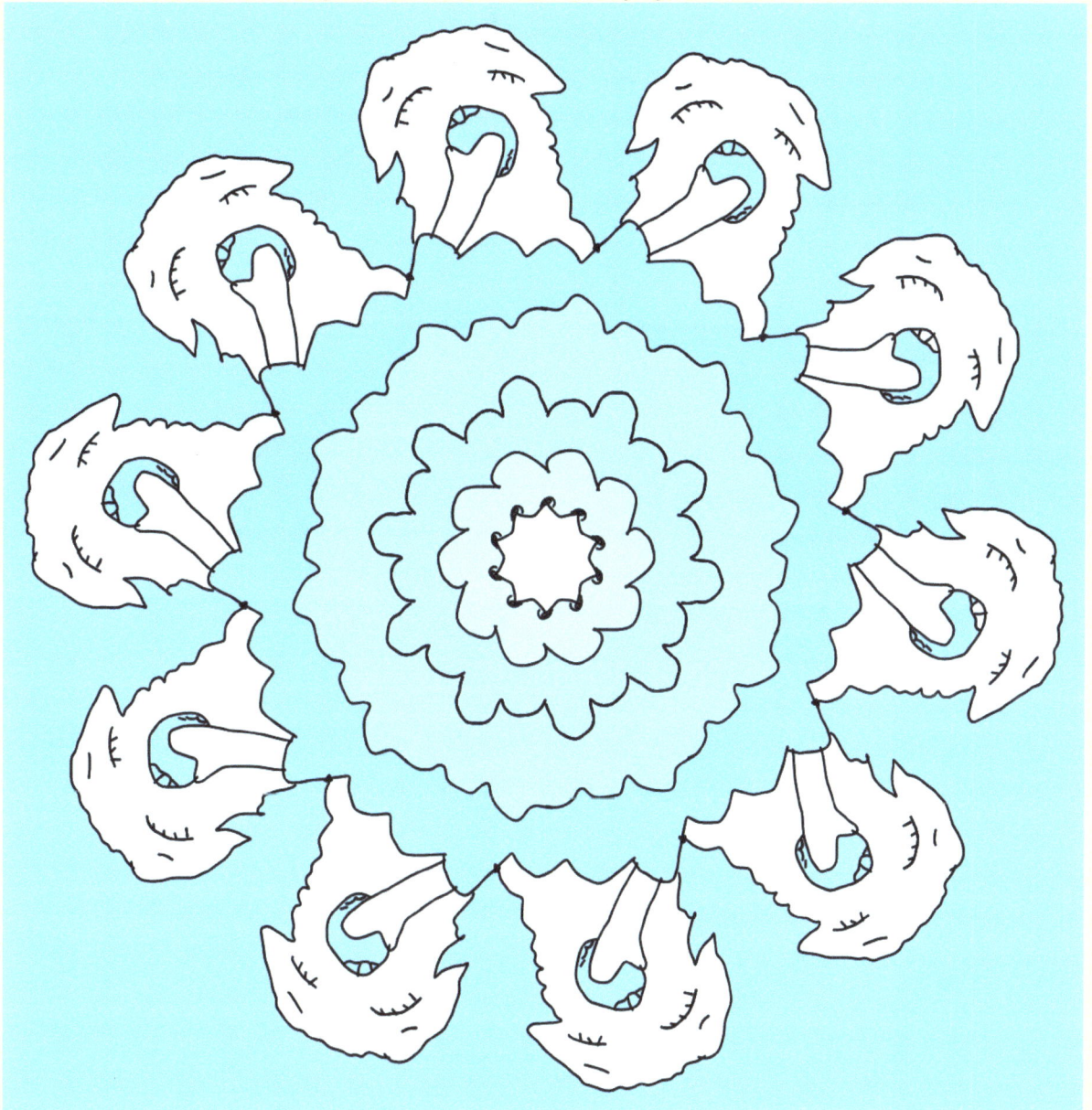

What happens inside to make you look sleepy?

This mandala expresses someone's feelings. It has dots and triangles.

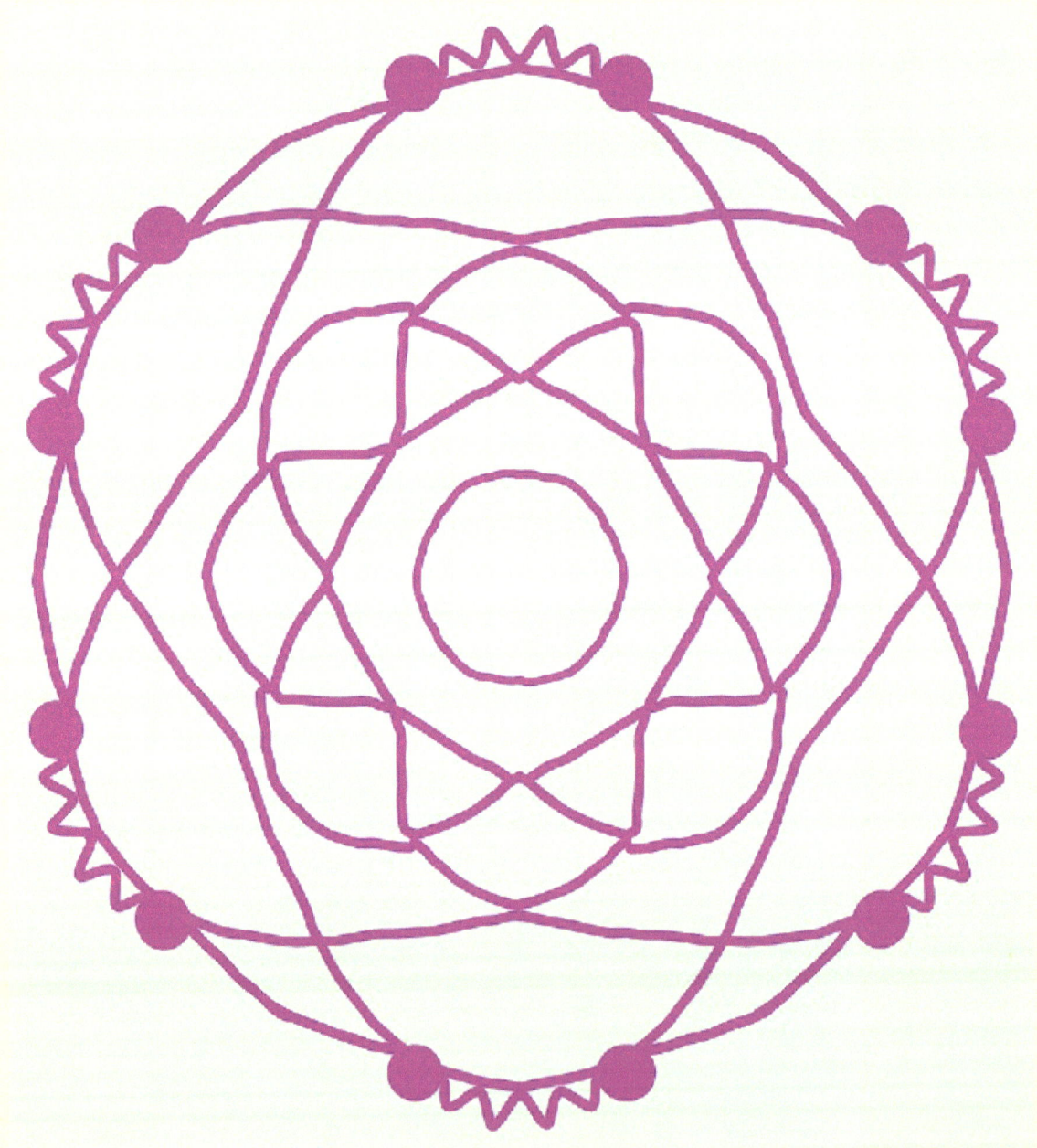

Do your feelings have shapes?

22

Can we feel yellow, red, blue, magenta, and pink?

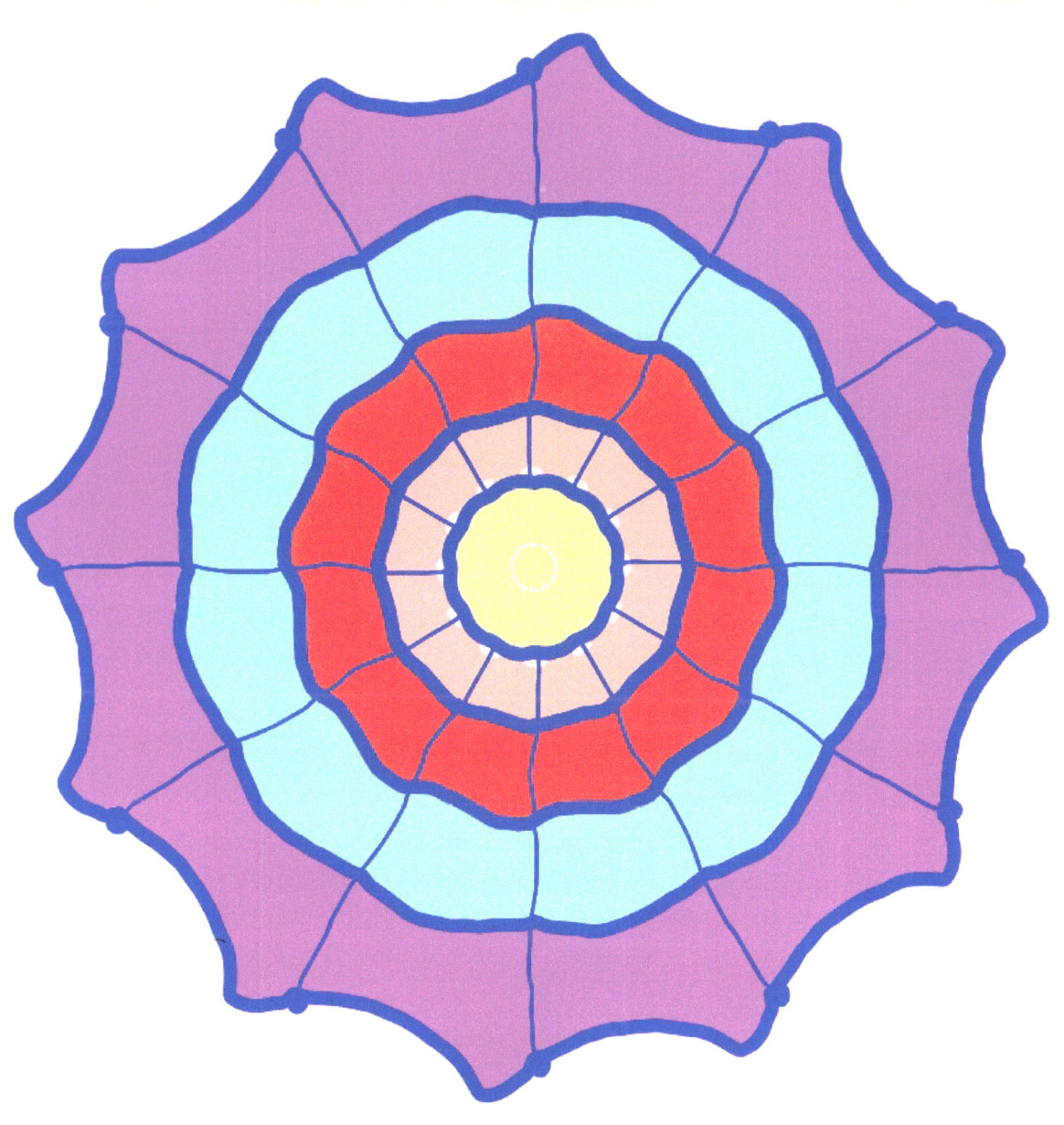

Do your feelings have colors?

Do people experience feelings like petals of a flower, or points on a snowflake?

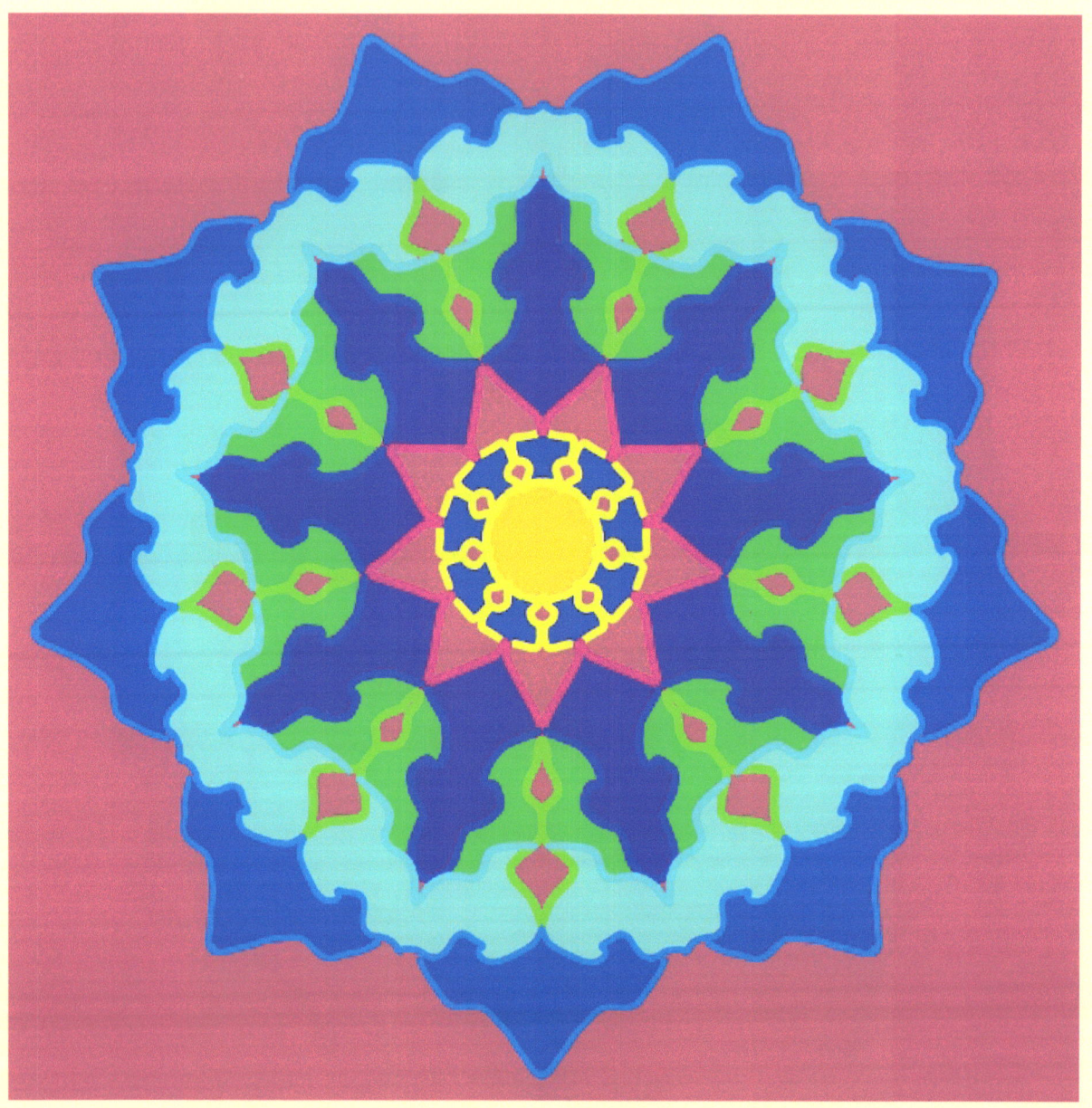

Do your feelings look like things you see in nature?

Sometimes when we look at a person on the outside.

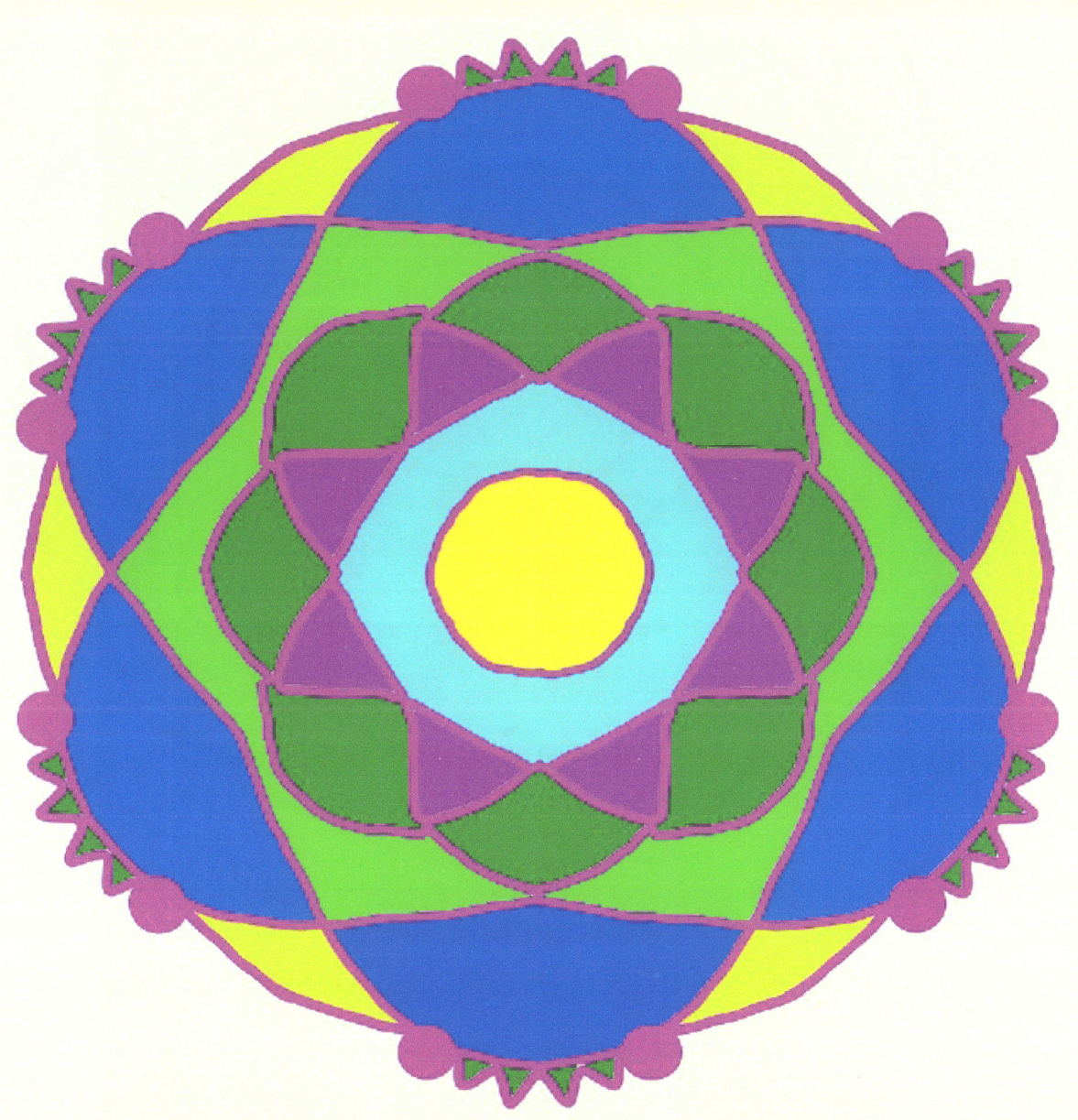

We can understand how they feel inside.

25

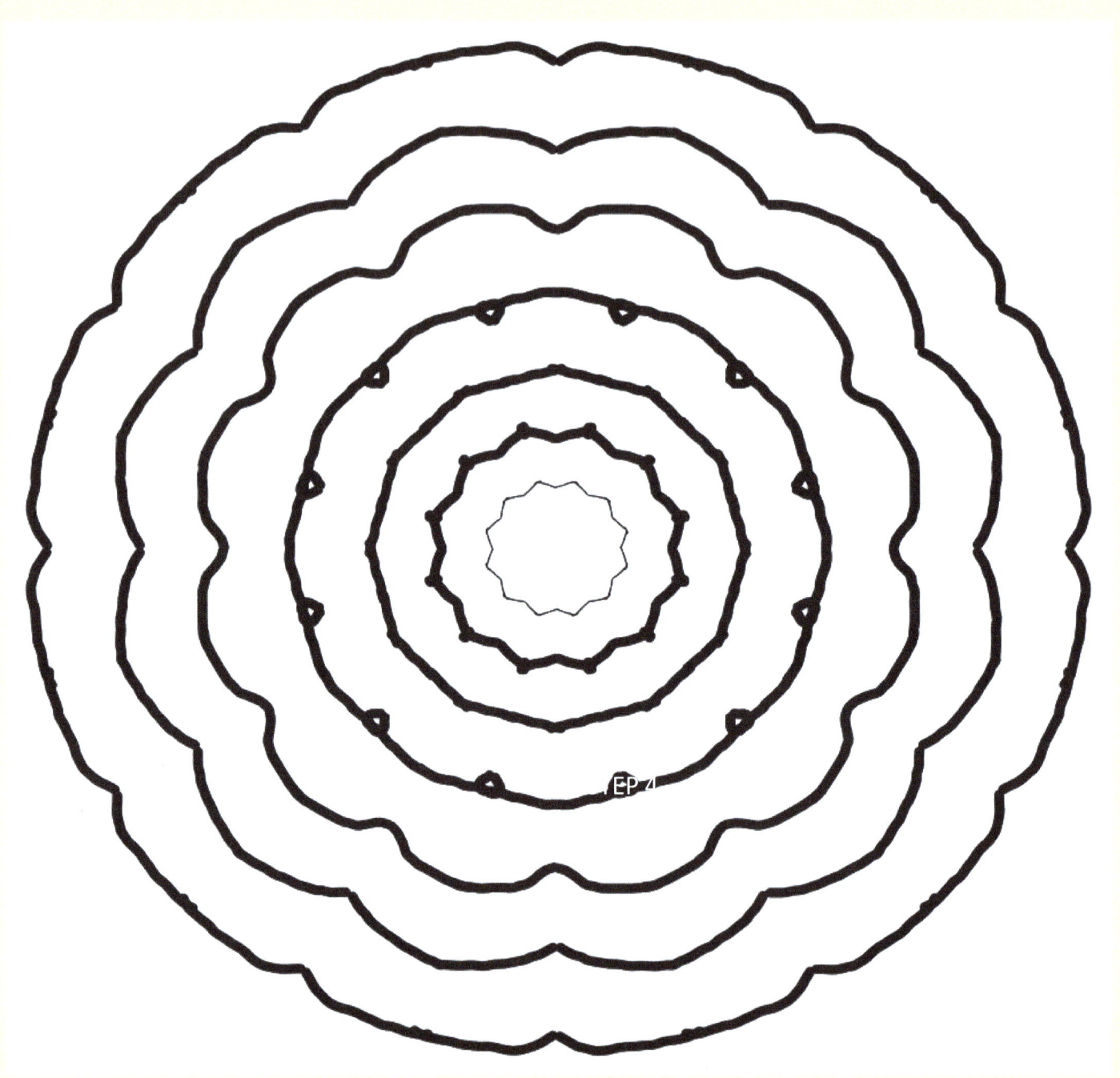

How would you draw, paint or color the feelings

you

have inside?

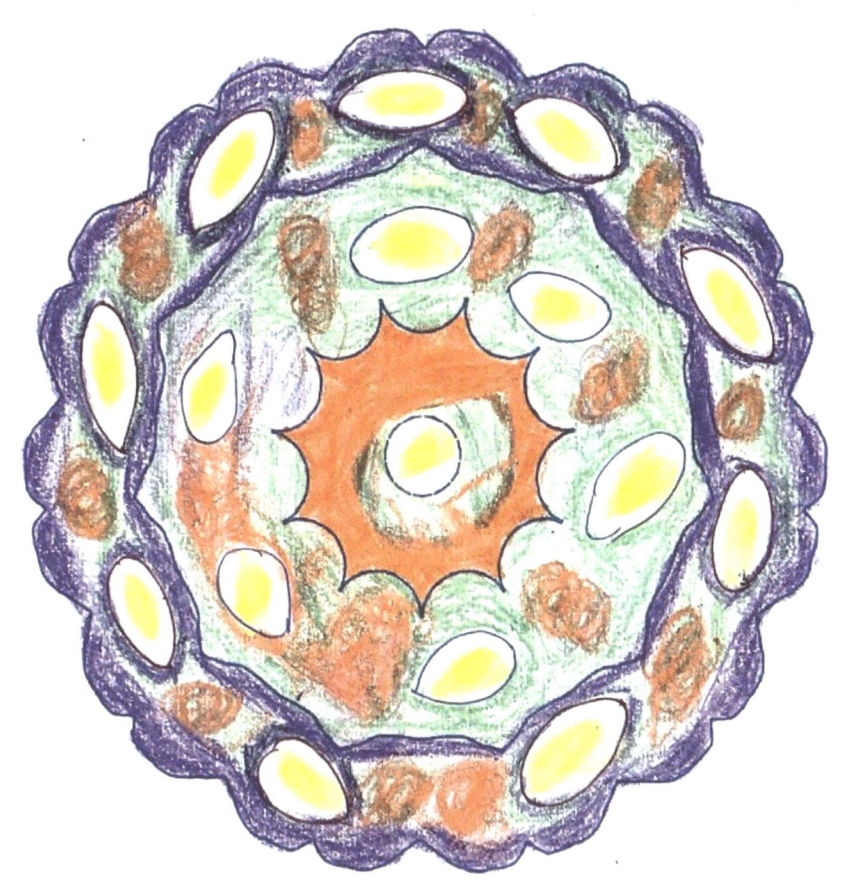

Example of completed mandala and how it can be used to encourage creative writing.

To the Voice

A voice.
Familiar?
Not so familiar.
Stirs excitement!
Brings newness, provokes hopefulness,
Inspires creativity, rekindles purpose, irritates slumber, and
Revives a desire to keep producing and living.
-Pedwis

ABOUT THE BOOK-

Creating Emotion Mandalas guides us to connect with and sense our internal emotional reality—and to express our emotions through an art form born of ancient mystical traditions. It is a way to give visual shape to the ineffable within us. With mandalas we now can build easier access to experiences that are exceedingly difficult to define meaningfully.

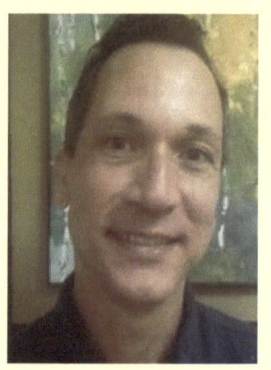

Jim Porter, Ph.D., LMHC

Emotional Intelligence builds when we learn to observe and allow our emotions to be what they are or change if they need to without trying to force them to be or change to what we think they should be.

Unconscious cognitive and bodily methods we use to dim emotions down and cut them off from awareness cloud awareness, and experience of our feelings can fade through persistently looking at our inner life. Personal emotion mandalas gently bring awareness of emotional vocabulary. This can be the beginning of the expression of our emotions which will start to loosen up the stuck, repetitive, impulsive thinking and behavior that we have been using for so long to block our emotions. This loosening in turn allows a more natural flow of emotion, allowing more choice in behaving and thinking.

Paradigms depict the internal life of human beings as a flow of behaviors, thoughts, and feelings. Throughout the history of psychology, there has been disagreement about which causes the other, or whether external stimuli cause the rest.

Now, science recognizes that all three influence each other—reciprocally. Our feelings influence our thoughts, our thoughts influence our behaviors, our behaviors influence our feelings, our feelings influence our behaviors, our behaviors influence our thoughts, and our thoughts influence our feelings. And yes, external stimuli are part of the picture, too.

Many traditional methods only target behaviors or thoughts, perhaps because it seems easiest to define and work with them. However, we are rediscovering that direct access to our emotions is possible. They can be addressed directly. The key often lies in building a sensory connection to, and expression of, emotions.

Finally, and importantly, it is either a truth, or a particularly useful construct, to say that things go much deeper—that we have a soul. Mandalas bring us back to this deeper place—to the to the discovery of You.

ABOUT THE AUTHOR/ ILLUSTRATOR-

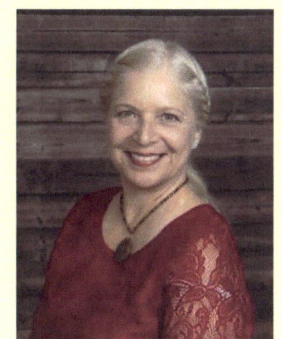

Karen White Porter is a Director of Loga Springs Academy and a Nationally Board-Certified Teacher. After graduating from Rutgers University with a Masters Degree in language education, she started teaching children. It was then that she realized the importance of emotional intelligence among her students. Having taught around the world gave her insight into to importance of the emotional underpinnings of how all people learn. She has taught at East China Normal University in Shanghai, P.R. China, Hofstra University in Hempstead N.Y., Hillside Public Schools in New Jersey, Saint Andrews University in Saint Andrews Scotland, Belcher Elementary in Clearwater Florida, The University of South Florida, The State University of Florida, and Loga Springs Academy.

ABOUT THE CO-AUTHOR-

Dr. Martha Marcella Joseph Watts, affectionately called "Aunty Marcella", is an author, English teacher, teacher trainer, and an independent educational consultant. She is best known for her Writing to Respond (WTR) process—an approach for guiding students in writing in response to what they read. She has published several educational resources to support implementation of the WTR process. These resources include books, workbooks, classroom charts, student, and educator wheels. She is also author of *The Adventures of Iyani* children's fiction series. Dr. Watts has taught on the elementary, secondary and university levels and has done so in her home country of Dominica, in the US Virgin Islands, and in Florida. Her interaction with students in diverse settings gives her the opportunity to observe students' emotional reaction to natural disasters, school unrest, and personal loss in unique ways.

www.ingramcontent.com/pod-product-compliance
Lightning Source LLC
Chambersburg PA
CBHW041936240526
45473CB00034B/1717